Decorate for Living

Phyllis Sloan Allen tells how to

Decorate for Living

Brigham Young University Press

The universal charm of clean-cut lines, warm colors, hardwood floors, and soft rugs is demonstrated in the room on the cover. Well arranged space, with comfortable and well placed furniture, add to its appeal. Carefully chosen and arranged accessories complete the inviting room. *Courtesy of Drexel Heritage Furnishings.*

Printed in the United States of America
by Brigham Young University Printing Service
4 79 20Mp 38220

Library of Congress Cataloging in Publication Data

Allen, Phyllis Sloan.
Decorate for living.

Includes index.
1. Interior Decoration—Handbooks, manuals, etc.
I. Title.
NK2110.A53 747'.8'83 79-1228
ISBN 0-8425-1627-1

Contents

dedicated to anyone
and everyone interested
in creating a home

Introduction

For too long, too many Americans have strained, through acquiring "things," to achieve the supposed status of their more affluent peers. The time is far overdue for each of us to reevaluate our lives—to weigh how we are *trying* to live against how we can *afford* to live, and to set some sensible and realistic priorities based on our resources and our own way of life.

Even before history began, man's need for shelter had to be satisfied in one way or another. Some of the earth's earliest inhabitants were content with the natural shelter of the cave. But soon primitive human beings began to fashion various kinds of enclosures. These dwellings provided only the barest necessities of life. Then, as civilizations evolved, the desire for bodily comfort brought about constant refinements—not only in the basic structure of the dwelling itself, but also in interior components. Thus, visual beauty in the dwelling was considered desirable long before today's so-called necessities.

The most recent development is the *study* of the interior environment, particularly its psychological impact. And today's environmental scientists emphasize that the home environment has a dramatic impact on attitudes and character development during the formative years. Therefore, every homemaker should set as top priority the need for creating a home in which the functional, aesthetic, and spiritual needs of all household members are satisfied.

The key to successful home decorating is suitability. But what suits one family may not suit another. If a house suits a family and serves its true function, it will fill the needs of every family member. A *house* begins with wood, brick, and mortar. A *home* begins with people, and *your* home must begin with *your* people and their needs. Consider first: How do you live? What are your interests and hobbies? Don't concern yourselves unduly with how others live. Your home is for you, your family, and *your* way of life. To copy what someone else does is to pretend. Pretense is transparent and does not impress anyone. "Keeping up with the Joneses" has caused far too much frustration, financial burden, and unhappiness, and should have been outmoded long ago.

Moreover, furnishing a home can be one of life's real pleasures, and each step should be enjoyed. Good decorating is made up of many factors: taste, value, style, comfort, convenience, individuality, and a good measure of common sense. Decorating is the art of creating a personal environment shaped by tangible elements through the application of intangible principles. There is no such thing as instant decorating. No matter how casual a room may look, if it is successful it will show evidence of studied effort and mature judgment.

Building a house takes a few months, but decorating a home is an on-going process. As families change, their needs change, and finding solutions to these changing needs is a constant challenge. Modern technology can solve many physical problems within the house, but we must avoid excesses and must always place hûman values in top priority.

Today's most critical housing need is space. But before you despair of being able to afford more space, be sure you are getting the most from the space you already have. In all home furnishings be aware of the planned obsolescence that often cheapens design and workmanship. If what you have is good, don't discard it; fix it up and use it. Anticipate your needs and become an intelligent consumer. Look for good design in a price you can afford, and always shop with the future in mind.

Based on the many questions I have been asked by today's homemakers, this book is my best effort to present practical ideas in clear terms. I hope that within these pages the homemaker—male or female, single or married—will find the incentive to study and create an environment that shows good taste and a distinctly individual character, and will learn that ideas—not dollars—make the biggest difference.

Now, more than ever before, our country needs the strength and stability of the home to maintain and foster the values upon which the nation was established. We ought to set as top priority the responsibility of creating home environments in which the values of honesty, integrity, tolerance, understanding, and respect are nurtured and preserved. And with the mounting pressures of modern life, it is probably more important today than ever before that our homes be true havens, providing a feeling of serenity and well-being for all who dwell there. Again, such an environment does not happen by accident; it requires intelligent planning and constant revision. It is this environment that makes the difference between a house and a home.

1
A Face-Lift for a House

So you want to redecorate your house? You are sick and tired of the same old things and everything is getting shabby and run down. But what to do? All you hear these days are complaints about the outrageous prices of everything and the difficulty of getting reliable workmen to do small jobs. You can believe it, for heaven knows how hard it is to get a plumber to unplug a toilet, and when he finally gets it done, the cost is enough to bring on a major heart attack.

Or perhaps what you really want is a new house; but with the exorbitant prices of groceries, clothes, and utilities, not to mention medical bills and other expenses, a new house is out of the question. Actually, you may find that the house you have is quite adequate. There may be things you don't like about it; but with a few minor changes and a face-lift, it should get you by for a few more years. By then, your needs may have changed. You may even want a smaller place. You never know. But you can take care of that when the time comes. In the meantime, you have a job to do, decisions to make, and a home to make as attractive and livable as possible.

Maybe the place wouldn't really be too bad if things were fixed up. That dining room set you bought at an auction is still sturdy. The seats need recovering, but the style looks pretty good. Seems like you saw one similar to it in a recent newspaper advertisement. You wonder what style it is, or if it *has* a style? You have never really bothered to find out. Perhaps you *ought to.* You wonder if it is worth refinishing? What would it cost? Maybe you could do it yourself? You have never done any refinishing, but there is a first time for everything. You could give it a try.

You speculate that the person who planned your house must have been a woman hater. Just to keep this open space fit for habitation takes constant picking up and straightening around—not to mention the scratched furniture, frayed upholstery, and worn path in the carpet caused by constant through traffic.

"Why is it," you ask yourself, "that the Kawasakis' house doesn't have the same rundown look mine has?" Is it because their house has an entrance hall that keeps most of the traffic out of the living room? Or because the entrance has a tile floor instead of carpet? That tile has been down ever since they moved in; it still looks like new; and you never see them cleaning it. Much of their furniture is old, older than yours in fact. Why does it look so much better? Your living room is more modern than theirs. Why does shabby modern furniture seem to look so much worse than other shabby furniture?

And then there is Carol with all of her nice things and living in a house that always looks ready for company. And Fred. Oh yes, Fred, who is always adding on a room or getting new furniture and drapery.

This questioning and comparing could go on and on, but what good does it do? Why should you fret about other peoples' houses and what they have in them? It's *your* house and *your* family that should concern you. But where do you begin?

How do you go about improving your house these days without an excessive outlay of money? How do you decide on just what to buy? You've looked through scores of those decorating magazines without relating to any of the rooms you have seen. They are too jumbled up, too faddish. Certainly they wouldn't do for *your* family. Besides, most of the changes would cost too much. You see numerous references to an interior designer and the wonders she can work. It all sounds very nice, but this, too, is an expense you cannot afford. Where *do* you start? How do you begin to make your house your home?

Begin at the Beginning

Don't despair! Just begin at the beginning. And where is the beginning? First of all, take an objective look at your house, overall and in detail. Try this. Walk a block away, then turn around and approach your house as though you were a stranger and had never seen it before. Are you completely pleased with what you see?

How does the planting look? Are the shrubs overgrown and in need of pruning or replacing? Are they placed in a way that enhances the lines of the house, or are they planted hit and miss, with utter disregard for "design"? Does the house generally look well-kept, or does it look a bit neglected? Does it need repainting? Is the roof in need of repair? What about the windows, the "eyes" of the house? Are they treated uniformly from the inside, or does one have ruffled tiebacks, another a venetian shade, and still another conspicuously colored drapery? If there are shutters or awnings, are they in a state of disrepair with a few slats missing and paint that is peeling?

Now look at the front door—the focal point of your house. Is the door really right for the house? Is it neatly stained or painted? Is the hardware appropriate and well polished? Are the side lights right for the style of the house, correctly placed and sparkling clean? Would a potted plant or two add a friendly note?

Step back a moment and take another long look. Are there some things still to be desired? Do you want to be judged by what you see? If you are less than satisfied, make some notes for use in your "plan" later on.

Now open the front door. What is the picture that confronts you? Do you see a matted path in the shag rug leading from the door across the living room through the dinette area and to the exposed kitchen? Is everything in full view: the dining table piled with a conglomeration of family drop-downs, shoes on the floor, a jacket draped over a chair, a tennis racket leaning against the television, and a variety of miscellaneous items scattered thither and yon: If so, you are probably a victim of the architects and house planners of the 1930s through 1950s who were advocating the so-called functional plan and telling people that they didn't need entrance halls. Wasted space, they said. They also said families didn't need dining rooms. Wasted space! So homeowners went along with them. And homeowners still tend to do the "in" thing.

Why are we so gullible? Why don't we dare speak up for what we want and know we need in our homes? Why do we allow ourselves to be dictated to by someone who knows and cares little about the things in a house plan that are necessary to carrying on the day-to-day activities with a minimum of friction.

The Movement Toward Remodeling

It took a while, but eventually families rebelled against these "functional" houses and started looking for older homes with livable space. Thus began the movement toward buying and recycling old houses. In re-

What was once a breezeway becomes a workshop for a garden and houseplant enthusiast. The bonus is a home-study center. Alabaster white and daffodil yellow provide a cheerful atmosphere. *Courtesy of Ethan Allen.*

cent years, scores of families have relocated and are loving their new-found freedom as well as the luxury and convenience of well-planned space.

In the 1960s this movement became evident to some of the building industries and to the editors of *House and Garden.* In their concern they made a nationwide survey asking American women what they really wanted in their houses. The survey revealed that women all across the country were unhappy with the open-planned house that had been thrust upon them. They expressed this in their common plea to get back to houses that would meet the needs of families. They wanted an entrance hall, a dining room, a pantry, separate rooms for children, and a living room off bounds to pets and peanut butter.

The reaction to the survey resulted in a positive response on the part of many architects and builders. Now houses are getting back to basics. Not, however, before homeowners lived through years of frustration trying to adapt their lives and the lives of their families to houses that were called functional, but were proven to be anything but that.

During recent years, there has been a remarkable change in floor plans and in houses. The trend is back to building up instead of out. The two-story house, once almost standard for families, is back in favor. It takes up less ground, requires only half the roofing, saves energy in both heating and cooling, and can provide great flexibility of space for all family needs. In light of the high cost of real estate, building materials, and utilities, this trend makes sense.

Thoughts on Face Lifting

Now let us get back to the survey of your own house and the view that confronted you as you entered your front door. How can these problems be remedied without a major remodeling project? With very little expense, you could *create* a foyer. It may not be perfect, but at least it will give you a little privacy and improve the initial impression on your visitors.

There are a number of ways to create a foyer or entryway, depending upon the size of the room, the placement of the outside door, and the arrangement of the rooms to be reached. Where space is very limited, a free-standing screen can do the trick. It takes almost no space, can be high enough to provide privacy, and yet not cut out light. A bonus will be a backdrop in the living area for a furniture grouping.

A free-standing screen creates an entry and provides a backdrop for furniture.

One of the most successful ways to set off an entrance is by the use of a storage divider. The divider will require two to three feet of space, but it may be planned with numerous storage combinations, depending on your needs. For example, it may provide space for wraps on the entry side and open bookshelves on the living room side. This type of divider can be decorative as well as functional. Whatever the size or type of divider you choose, the design should be in keeping

The privacy provided and the storage gained more than compensate for loss of space.

with the general feeling of your house. You will find that the advantages gained and the satisfaction you will find in this simple change will more than compensate for the small amount of floor space lost.

But maybe you already have an entrance hall. If you have, how does it look? Is it a bit dreary? Start with the floor. Does it need recarpeting? Better still, why not be practical and have beauty at the same time. The market abounds with attractive hard surface materials of all types and descriptions defying hard wear and requiring little upkeep.

What about the walls? Are they drab? Visualize what a dramatic wallpaper could do to bring new life into the room. A three-dimensional mural could push out one wall and make the small space appear twice as wide. Putting it on is no problem. You can do it your self.

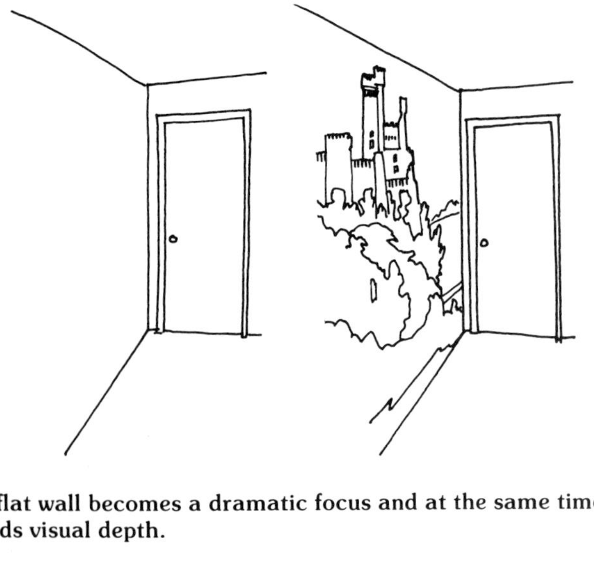

A flat wall becomes a dramatic focus and at the same time adds visual depth.

A handsome divider provides storage space as well as privacy for eating and relaxing away from kitchen clutter. *Courtesy of Armstrong Cork Co.*

The chair you have there could do with a new seat cover. A small remnant will do. That table is too large and obstructs traffic. How many times have you struck your hip bone on it as you rounded the corner in a hurry? One of those little wall-hung shelves may be just the answer. The mirror already there could be used to better advantage.

What about the lighting? Does it provide adequate light for greeting guests, or is the ceiling light too small and nondescript? Well! You've made a start. What do you think? Now go through each room in your house and do the same thing you did in your entrance. Take time to look critically, first at the overall appearance, then at each item. Make careful notes. When you have finished, sit down, put your feet up, take a deep breath, and relax. You have taken the first and most important step toward a complete face lift of your house.

Your Primary Objective—A Home that Reflects Your Way of Living

The next big step is to make a plan; but before you do this, get a few things well established in your mind. Decide what you want your house to look like when you are through. What is the look that most nearly reflects your family's life style? Is it elegant, country, rustic, or modern? Do you yearn for elegance, but have misgivings about its practicality with your active family? What is elegance? True elegance is *simplicity*. It is common sense expressed naturally and with no pretense. It must be an honest expression of your own way of life. If you try to imitate the life style of someone else, it will be apparent because your home will be devoid of your personality. If your home is to be successful, it must reflect your own individuality and the individuality of all those who live there.

What is individuality? It is something that cannot be purchased, and it is never the same—not even for two people. It is intangible, and yet very real. It is that elusive undefinable quality that we should all be seeking to establish in our homes. That quality which, more than any other, makes your home peculiarly yours—individuality is what makes the difference.

How to Achieve Your Objective

"But," you ask yourself, "can I achieve all this?" The answer is, "Yes, you can." You can if you have the desire, the patience, and the willingness to study and work hard. You can have a home with charm and good taste—*and on a limited budget.* If you are willing to follow a few guide lines, the task ahead will be made infinitely more successful.

- Develop your artistic taste. Train your eye to be "aware", to recognize beauty in simplicity, and to learn to create beauty with commonplace things. Always keep in mind that fashion is not a good criterion of design. As with clothes, fashion in home furnishings may become outdated. Remember that if any item in your home, from a teaspoon to a piano, exemplifies good design when it is purchased, *it will always be good.* (See chapter 5.)
- Learn how to make the most of space. Study the principles of spatial design. Decide what *you* use your rooms for—not what other people use their rooms for. Plan each room on paper where moving furniture is easy. This will not tell the whole truth about furniture arrangement, but it will be very helpful. Remember that rooms should be livable as well as lookable. (See chapter 12.)
- Learn about color. Remember that it is the most important and the least costly of all the decorative elements, that there is no such thing as a bad color if it is used in the right quantity, value, and intensity and in the right environment, and remember that what colors do to each other is of the greatest importance. (See chapter 6.)
- Discover the magic of fabric. Be knowledgeable about new fibers and fabrics. Learn some simple guidelines about combining patterns and textures. Discover what kinds of fabrics are appropriate for particular styles and moods. Decide upon the effect you want in your rooms, then create that effect with the suitable fabric. (See chapter 7.)
- Become an intelligent shopper. Keep abreast of new materials; but before making a purchase, be sure that each item has been thoroughly tested. Be aware of new trends in furniture styles, but keep in mind that the quality of design, whether it be in a house, a piece of furniture, or a small accessory, is never determined by age. Good design is always good. (See chapters 8 and 11.)
- After much careful study and observation, when you feel reasonably qualified to discriminate between good and bad, have the courage of your convictions. Don't be afraid to project your own personality into your home. Remember, your house is for you to live in, not for others to approve. Always keep in mind that the most important ingredient in setting the atmosphere of your home is *you.* (See chapters 13–14 and 16–18.)

Whether you are starting to furnish your first apartment, redoing a single room, or redecorating an entire house, remember that it is the idea and not the dollar that is the most important. Use your imagination and plan to do as much of the work yourself as possible. There are do-it-yourself kits listed in most decorating magazines. Today's homemaker is no longer circumscribed by the rules in effect at the turn of the century. So relax and enjoy fixing up your house, and remember that charm is not dependent on income. Wealth may even hinder the expression of good taste because it invites ostentation, and this does not make a home where families can live happily and function at their best.

2
New Home -- Old Address

When your most critical housing need is space, redecorating alone will not solve your problem. If building a new house is out of the question, you may consider buying a bigger house—which also may be out of your financial reach—or remodeling the one you have. Maybe with some readjusting of the areas you have and adding on where it is mechanically and financially feasible you could acquire the space you so desperately need.

Today, hundreds of thousands of Americans are looking for more living space. But with spiraling building costs, a new home is out of reach for many families. Today's answer to the pressing need for space is a decided shift toward remodeling.

There are two alternatives to remodeling: enlarging and fixing up the home you are living in, or buying an older house to remodel. The decision requires careful study and there are many aspects to be considered. Whichever you decide to do, the problems, as well as the rewards of remodeling, are many. Sometimes the simplest improvement can add space and give a house new character, as well; but often, especially with older houses, a major overhaul is necessary and may involve a large expenditure. To encourage the renovation of older buildings, many local banks and governments provide low-cost financing as an incentive.

Why Remodel Your Present House

When people who are planning to remodel are asked, "Why not just sell and get another house?" the most important reasons they give are not economic, but social and emotional. The most frequently cited reasons for staying where they are include: liking the community and the established neighborhood, having cherished memories of growing up in the area, being strongly attached to trees and gardens nurtured over

A structurally sound home restored to its original beauty. *Courtesy of San Francisco Victoriana Designers and Builders.*

many years, enjoying personal and family ties in the local environment, and being unwilling to face the hassle of moving and trying to adjust to another place.

Why Buy An Old House to Remodel

One reason that people buy old houses to remodel is the widespread feeling of nostalgia that was fostered during the bicentennial year. This, combined with the need for space, has brought old houses into great demand. Many of the houses built around the turn of the century were meant to last forever; they are still structurally sound; and their high ceilings, beautiful wood trim, and plank floors, deep windows, and ample, well-arranged space are a joy to today's families. Another nice thing about these houses is that no two are alike.

Although much maligned for many years, these houses hold a strange magic for many people. Never was a house so beloved by children as the Victorian. It was built with big families in mind and can take the everyday knocks of living without leaving a trace. The back and front stairways, with their sturdy banisters, make a marvelous slide. The numerous little nooks and crannies are wonderful for hiding or just for being alone and day dreaming. And for watching the world go by, or the rain spattering on the neighbor's roof, there is often a special cupola way up on top.

As these Victorian houses fell into disrepute, thousands fell to the bulldozer, making those remaining harder and harder to find. But the recent wave of preservation in every state has brought their destruction almost to a halt. They are still to be had in almost every city and small town in the country, particularly in old and often run-down neighborhoods. If the persistent searcher is lucky, he or she may find one of these old beauties in an area where massive renovation is going on, thus recreating the once prestigious neighborhood.

Look to the attic. With a shoestring budget and a lot of imagination, unused space can become the favorite spot in the house. The only major purchase here was the love seat. The large wooden spool and director chairs serve many purposes. The old trunk and rocker are family treasures. *Courtesy of Linda and Dan Allen.*

Below: Here it is—"everybody's" old basement, not really right for anything. *Right*: With careful planning, minimal expense, and a few handy remedies for concealing the room's shortcomings, the basement becomes a family center for music and games. *Courtesy of Armstrong Cork Co.*

Before You Proceed

Whether your decision is to remodel your present home or to purchase and recycle an older house, don't proceed until you have done much careful study and investigation. Before embarking on a major remodeling project, look into the building codes in your area. Everywhere there are zoning restrictions in what you can and cannot do, so these should be clarified at the outset.

The next step is to make a preliminary survey of the house. It would be wise to have a reputable contractor or some knowledgeable person assist you. If you have just purchased the house and are new in the community, ask the building inspector to recommend a reliable person. Together, make an exhaustive survey, starting with the foundation. Check carefully for soundness, cracks and water seepage. Check the walls, floors, and roof framing. If all of these are structurally sound, the house is probably worth rehabilitating. Then, with the contractor, inspect the heating, plumbing, and electrical systems. If he puts his "OK" on these, you should feel reasonably confident in proceeding.

But there are other danger points that need to be checked before you make a firm commitment. Check the following:

Checklist for Structural Problems

1. Are there cracks in the chimney brickwork?
2. Is the flashing loose, missing, or defective?
3. Are the gutters decayed from clogging?
4. Where clapboard meets the trim, is it tight or is it rotted from water?
5. Are downspouts sufficiently large to carry off all water?
6. How is the mortar between bricks? Is it soft, crumbling, in need of repainting?
7. Is rot developing in the cornices?
8. Are there cracks in brickwork from uneven settling of the foundation?
9. Are window frames and sills in good condition?
10. Is there any evidence of termites at ground level?

All these problems can be spotted easily by a professional, and usually they can be corrected with minor repairs. Taking care of them immediately is important since it can prevent unexpected and costly problems in the future.

Do You Need an Architect

If your project is a major one, involving partitions and requiring additions, the question arises, should you engage an architect? This, of course, will involve more expense; but in the long run it may be wiser and even more economical.

But before you contact an architect, calculate realistically what you can spend and be sure to plan on its costing more than you think it will. It will! Go over your house carefully to determine what changes you plan to make. Do you need a room added on or partitions removed or installed to divide a bedroom or redirect traffic? Do you need closets built in or possibly an upper floor finished or even added on? Whatever your needs, lay them out on paper the best you can and live with them for a while. Remember that the purpose of your remodeling is to improve your living space. Be sure you accomplish this.

The surest way of getting what you want from your architect is to be able to present your plans in a clear, precise, intelligent manner. The architect will be grateful, because his reward is a satisfied client. If you don't know what you want and turn the entire project over to him, chances are you will be unhappy with the final result. Remember that although an architect must be skilled in engineering and drafting, he is first a designer and an artist, and if you don't direct him, his creative urge may take precedence over his concern for function and convenience. The responsibility of getting what you want rests with *you*. Your architect will see that the job is soundly engineered, but it is up to you to see that traffic lanes, openings, storage, and wall space are planned to meet your needs. Don't be afraid to speak up. A demanding, intelligent client is appreciated by a conscientious architect.

Who Will Do the Work

Now, who is going to do the work? Of course, the biggest saving is in doing the work yourself. This should be determined by the extent of the project and your own skill, as well as your personal interest and motivation. It would be wise to discuss this with an architect, too. He will advise you on what you can and cannot do successfully. If the job is more than you can tackle alone, the answer is a contractor. If you haven't one in mind, inquire of friends who have had similar work done. Or, contact a building firm or a building inspector—they can be helpful in suggesting someone reliable. It is becoming more and more difficult to find workmen who are willing to take on small personalized jobs, but they are still to be found. It is important to have a contractor whom you trust and with whom you can communicate.

Be sure the contractor you are considering has a state license and carries insurance for workmen's compensation, property damage, and liability. Before work begins, discuss the job thoroughly. Ask questions and express any fears or apprehensions you may have. When you feel comfortable with the contractor you have chosen, draw up a firm contract. It should include a detailed description of all work to be done, the approximate date of completion, and the schedule of payments. Your contract also should include a clean-up by the contractor when the job is completed.

You can save money by having the work done during a time other than the peak building season. The time may not be so convenient for you, but the financial saving may be worth it. Ask your contractor about this. He will give you a lower price if he can do your job when he is not under pressure.

The secret to successful and rewarding remodeling is in doing as much of the work as possible yourself. But before starting, outline the entire project. Remodeling without a carefully worked-out plan usually means waste and frustration. Don't try to do it all at once. Do the most critical areas first. Sure you will have a mess, inconvenience, frustrating delays, and you will likely make a few mistakes—which, by the way, can often be turned into assets—but if you anticipate these in advance, the whole project will go much smoother. Stay away from tricks and gimmicks, concentrate on quality and permanence, and in the end it will have been well worth it all. The final result should be a house to be proud of, with the space you need, whether it is a recycled house you bought or your "new" home at the old address.

3

Start with a Plan

Once you have reached the decision to remodel your present home, you have taken the first big step. The second step is to lay out a plan. In making your overall plan, you may find it beneficial to think as if you were starting a house from scratch. Lay out the most desirable space arrangement for your family, then see how nearly you can arrive at this in your remodeling with a minimum of structural change. Time and experience have proven that there are basic things in the general plan of a house that are conducive to the smooth working of a family home. Individual differences in the manner of living must always be taken into account, but basic, time-tested requirements should be incorporated into the planning of every home if it is to function efficiently.

The Importance of Well-Arranged Space

That the physical home environment has an impact upon peoples' lives is generally accepted today, but the importance of the arrangement of space is not fully recognized. Too often an impressive facade takes precedence, when actually it should be far down the list of requirements. The internal considerations of a house are of far greater importance than the exterior. Well-arranged floor space should be given top priority.

In getting the maximum advantage of limited space, well-planned traffic patterns are of major importance. Probably nothing in a home can fray a mother's nerves more than constant traffic from the front door through the living room and dining room to get to the kitchen and elsewhere. The irritations from this constant wear and tear and lack of privacy do not lessen but build up over the years. To have a home in which the many activities of today's families can be carried on with a minimum of frustration should be the major concern of every homemaker.

Changing the basic floor plan of an existing house is not usually feasible, but with the most essential re-

quirements in mind, minor changes can often correct some critical defects, thereby eliminating chronic annoyances.

Guidelines for an Efficient Floor Plan

Five basic requirements are necessary in a floor plan if it is to work efficiently for a family:

- Well-defined areas. There should be room for working, eating, family living for both relaxation and family activities, and areas for sleeping.
- Traffic lanes . . . adequate but not wasteful. A must is an entranceway that channels traffic to all areas of the house. There should be direct access from the kitchen to the front door, the back door, utility area, service area, and garage, easy access from one living area to the outside, and an access door into the garage near the front of the house (to permit children to get to the kitchen without going through the front door).
- Well-placed openings. Doors should be located to preserve wall space, and windows should be placed for easy draping—not up against a wall. Whenever possible, windows placed in bedrooms for cross-ventilation are desirable.
- Adequate wall space. The space should accommodate necessary pieces of large furniture.
- Ample storage conveniently located.
- Other Considerations. Plumbing should be economically located wherever possible, such as kitchen and utility room in close proximity, bathrooms back to back, plumbing in a second story placed directly above plumbing on the ground floor. A fireplace should be conveniently located for the arrangement of a private conversation area. When there are two fireplaces, they should be arranged to take advantage of the same chimney wherever feasible. Study and compare the floor plans on pages 16 and 17. Learn to read a blueprint. Becoming familiar with the architectural symbols on page 15 will also help.

Combine two fireplaces to share the same chimney where possible.

Left: Well-arranged space is conducive to pleasant living. A separate dining room provides privacy. A well-positioned fireplace becomes the focal point for a conversation area free from traffic in the contemporary home. *Courtesy of Syroco.*

Architectural Symbols

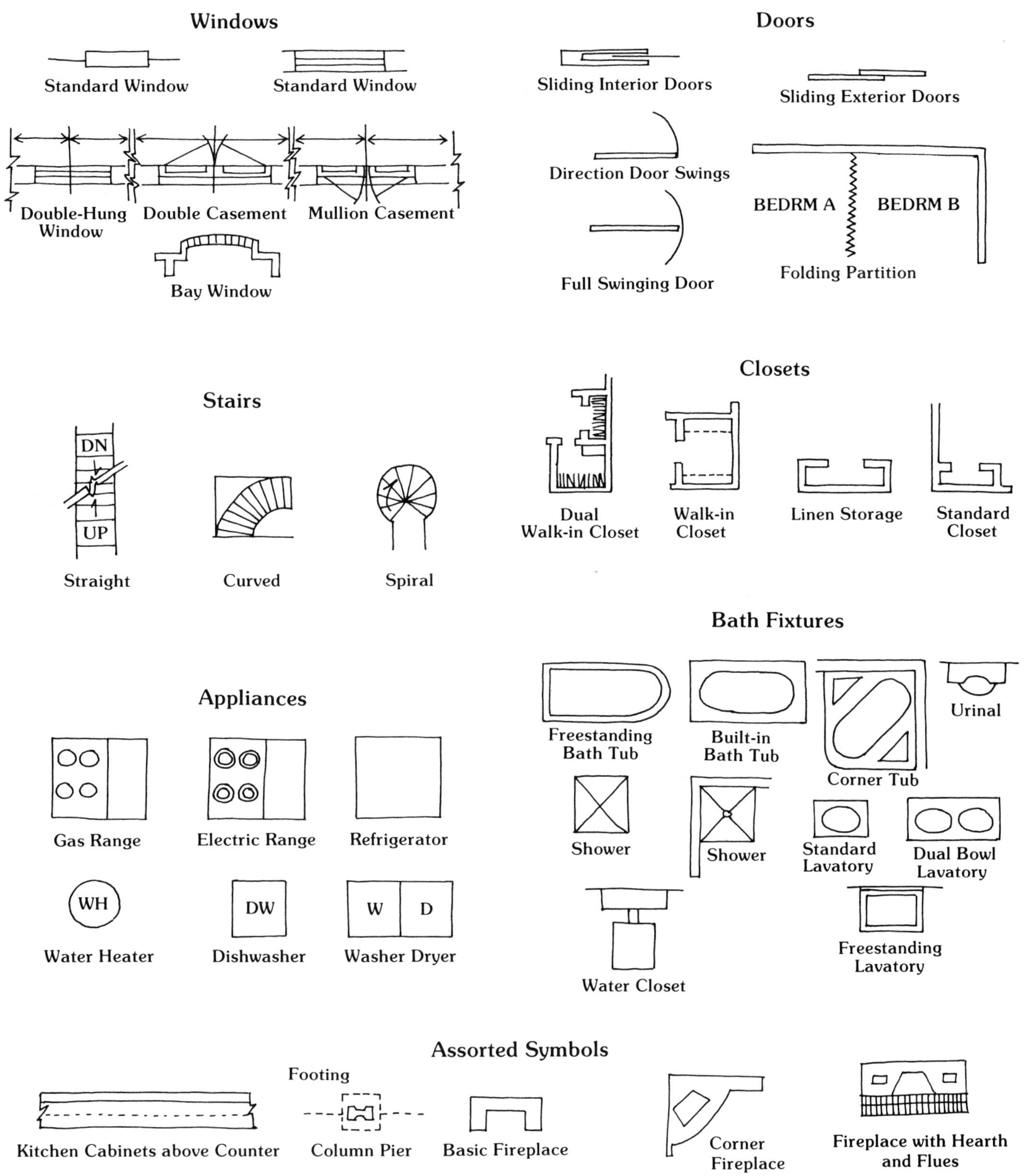

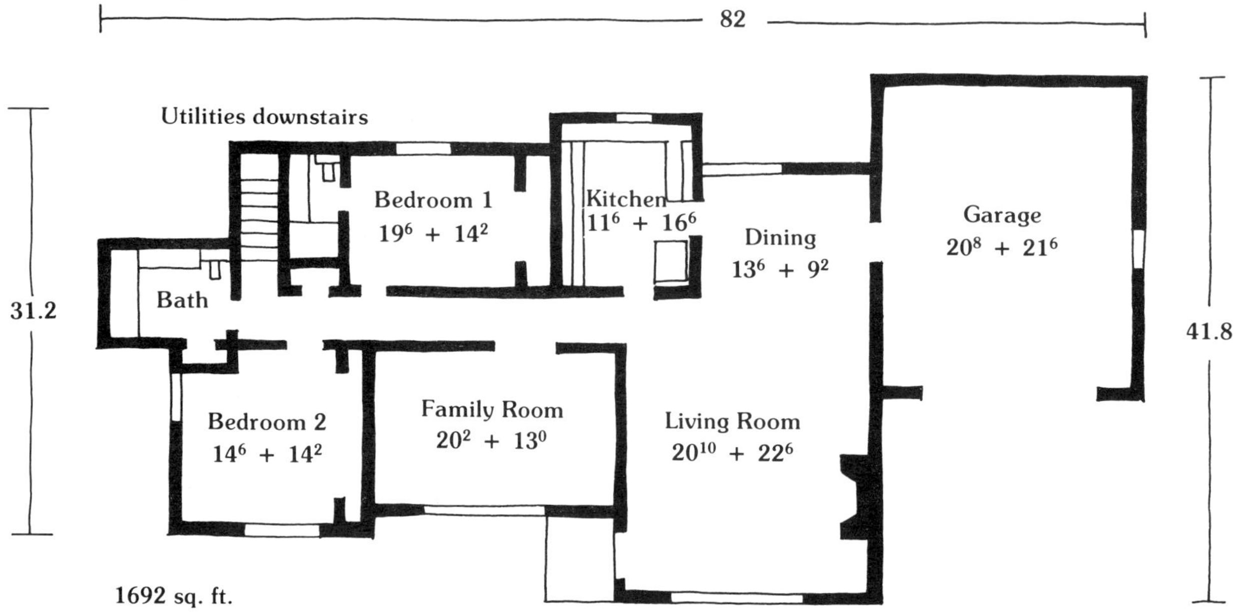

Poorly Arranged Floor Plan

Because of the poor arrangement of space in the above plan, the price per square footage would be unnecessarily costly, and living would be inconvenient and frustrating.

Undesirable Features

- There are too many costly jogs, twenty in all.
- The long hallway is a waste of space.
- Traffic lanes are not well planned:
  1. No space is provided for an entranceway into the front of the house, making the living room a major traffic lane.
  2. Eating space is limited, and the dining room is a major traffic lane between the garage and the kitchen, between the kitchen and the backyard, and between the kitchen and the front door.
  3. There is no access door into the front of the garage, from the garage to the backyard, nor from the family room to the outside.
- Utilities are in the basement, too far from the kitchen.
- The family room is too far from the kitchen.
- Bathrooms are not economically located.
- Windows in the corner bedroom and family room and the sliding doors in the dining area are butted against the wall, not allowing for drapery.
- There is no storage in the garage.
- The fireplace is poorly located for balance and for convenient conversation grouping.

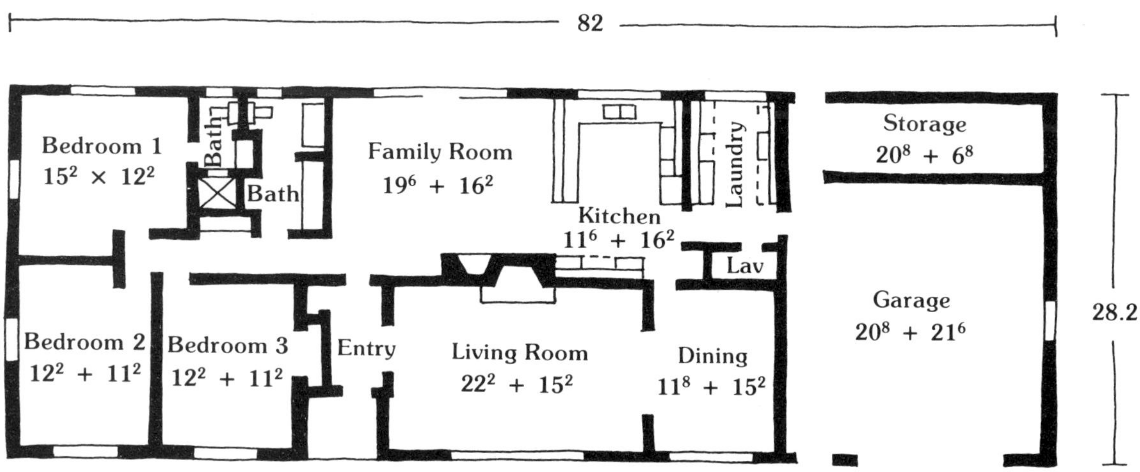

Well-Arranged Floor Plan

The revised and well-organized plan above with a third bedroom, additional storage, two fireplaces, and many other improvements could be built for less money than the preceding plan.

Improved Features

- Sixteen unnecessary jogs have been eliminated.
- A third bedroom has been added.
- The family room with outside entrance is open to the kitchen, with utilities placed near the kitchen.
- There is ample space for family eating, with a room for dining away from the kitchen.
- Traffic lanes are well planned:
  1. There are convenient traffic lanes from the kitchen to the outside.
  2. The entrance way directs traffic throughout the house.
  3. The living and dining rooms afford privacy.
  4. There is an outside entrance to the family room.
  5. There is an access door into the front of the garage and from the garage to the back yard.
- Plumbing is centralized: bathrooms in the bedroom wing are back to back—as are the kitchen and utilities.
- Windows in the corner bedroom and family room have been placed to allow for draping.
- Convenient storage is planned in the garage.
- A fireplace in the living room is placed for convenient conversation, and both fireplaces utilize the same chimney.

It may not be possible to incorporate all of these guidelines into your remodeling, but to approximate them as nearly as you reasonably can should prove beneficial.

We all need space to store and display our things. In this boy's room there is ample storage and surface space. The personally chosen wallpaper sets the mood for all manner of nautical objects—revealing individual interests. *Courtesy of Drexel Heritage Furnishings.*

Analyze Your Present Home

If your decision is to remodel your present home, carefully analyze it with the above guidelines in front of you. What are the things about it that have been the most annoying? Make a list of them and have each member of the household do the same. Include everybody's grievances. Have a session in which each person has a chance to voice his or her frustrations and to suggest solutions, keeping in mind that solutions should involve some "do-it-myself" suggestions. Don't overlook the good features of the house; list these also. Everyone will have to make concessions, but if problems and ideas are brought out and discussed together, it will be easier to set and agree upon priorities. Remember that the biggest money saver in your project will be your own ideas, imagination, and old-fashioned elbow grease.

Start with Family Hobbies

If your house serves its true function, it will fill the needs of all family members and not be merely attractively enclosed space to which they must adjust their lives. In laying out your particular plan, with guidelines in mind, start with *people—your* people and their hobbies and special interests. For example, if you have a photography buff, find a cubbyhole that can be turned into a darkroom. If some member of the household likes carpentry work, plan space for him in a garage or basement, preferably in a remote area, where noise will be muffled and interruptions cut to a minimum, and if possible, where there will be easy access to the back yard.

If someone sews, plan an area to contain the necessary items. The space need not be large if it is well organized. There must be a way to close it off easily and

Organization is the key to efficiency.

quickly when the person must leave in a hurry. Anyone who sews knows that an area used for this purpose is of little value if things have to be put away every time there's an interruption. The sewing area is one place in the house that has to be cluttery if it is to be useful.

What about pets? Is there a cat or a dog lover among you? If there is, this too should be taken into consideration. Cats shed hair, and their claws can wreak havoc with delicate fabrics. So if your cat has free run of the house, avoid frustration by choosing for the most vulnerable places fabrics that will not show hair and will withstand cat abuse. Vinyls are marvelous. If you have a dog that is allowed in the house, think about this when you are selecting carpets and upholstery fabrics. Chances are that your favorite curl-up spot is also the dog's favorite spot. What will you do about it? Furthermore, a big dog has a way of gently and indifferently knocking things over, so lamps, plant stands, and accessories should not be precariously situated. Small dogs have their own peculiar idiosyncracies and some provision should be made for them if people and pets are to live compatibly together.

When space for hobbies and pets has been carefully considered and settled, you are ready to solve some of the little problems of day-to-day living that often loom large over a period of time.

Anticipate the Realities of Day-to-Day Living

As an important part of your planning, anticipate the realities of everyday living and make some concession to them to avoid constant friction. For example, girls will wash out their hose and undies and hang them dripping somewhere, most anywhere, and usually to the annoyance of someone. So, build a place to hang them. It can be a small rack in the bathroom and as small as the space between two studs in the wall. The problem is solved.

The most used traffic lane in the house is from the most convenient outside door to the kitchen. Children will come in with friends, pets, and muddy feet and will head for the kitchen, so make sure there is a convenient door near the front of the house other than the main door—they will not go around to the back. (See floor plans on pages 16 and 17.)

When people come in from playing golf or tennis, they need a convenient place to put their clubs and rackets. You can be sure that they won't take them upstairs or down the hall to a closet. They will drop them on the nearest surface they see, so make a place near the door where these things can be dropped without cluttering up the house.

The fusing together of individual ideas within the bounds of good design will take much study, careful planning, and know-how; but the outcome can be highly rewarding. And when remodeling finally begins, each member will take a personal interest in the project and will be less inclined to complain about the inconveniences caused along the way. Some will even be more willing to pitch in and help.

A discussion of the work to be done by the household members is important. Painting, hanging paper, laying tile floors and carpet squares, refinishing furniture, building shelves, and numerous other jobs can be done satisfactorily—if not perfectly—at great financial savings.

When you have worked out a plan that contains practical solutions to your problems and have come up with many dollar-wise decorating ideas to revitalize and personalize the rooms in your house, you are ready to begin in earnest.

How Much Comfort Can You Afford

One of the most American features of our homes is comfort. How important is it to you and how much can you afford? Enjoying our body comforts is as American as "apple pie." We like our steak and onion rings, but we don't want the odor of the cooking lingering in the house. We want to live in an exciting city, but we don't want the noise and the polluted air. We like to go to the mountains, but we complain of the dry air, so we carry a humidifier. We enjoy being near the beach, but complain because the damp air gets into our bones and frizzes our hair. Wherever we are, we want and expect the indoor environment to be cool enough, warm enough, moist enough, dry enough, clean enough, fresh enough—and quiet too.

And today's technology can provide all this—at a price! For those who can afford it, nothing is too much to pay for total comfort. For the rest of us, we have what we can afford and complain about the rest.

How much can you afford for air conditioning that is becoming standard equipment today? Do you really need it? Many of the older, well-built houses can be very comfortable without it most of the time, if managed right. In summer, keep the hot air shut out during the day; and allow the cool air to ventilate through the house at night. In areas that are particularly humid and where nights remain hot, this will not work; but in many areas of the country it works remarkably well. Actually, this is the original air conditioning and doesn't cost a dime extra.

The Problem of Noise

One of the things that plague many people today, especially in urban areas and near airports, is noise. Controlling it is one of the major problems that architects encounter, particularly when doing commercial designs. But it is not only in commercial areas that noise is a problem. We are all confronting it to some extent, and it is having a negative impact on our lives.

There are a number of things we can do in our homes to help alleviate this problem, and it may be well to consider them when building or remodeling. Following are some things that will shut out or absorb noise: (1) Use close-fitting storm doors and windows that provide noise-insulating space. (2) Use double-paned window glass. (3) Put acoustic tile on ceilings. (4) Place clothes closets and storage shelves nearest the source of the noise. (5) Use wall-to-wall carpet. (6) Use carpet on walls nearest the noise source. (7) Use full, floor-to-ceiling drapery. (8) Use more upholstered furniture than wood.

Do You Need an Interior Designer

Can you do the redecorating job and do it right, or should you consult a professional designer? Maybe the thought of working with a designer frightens you a little and makes you feel inadequate rather than more enthusiastic. Would a designer want to do things his or her way, which may not suit your way of living? How would you find one? How much will it cost?

Designers come in two general categories: those who are part of a design firm or work independently and those affiliated with a home furnishing store or a department store. There are some advantages to having an independent designer. One is that the designer has a wide variety of sources and can save you time and foot work in locating materials. This type of trained designer usually has an hourly fee, which may be prohibitive.

Most good home furnishing firms have become interior design conscious in recent years and have regular designers on their staffs at no extra cost to the client. When you work with these designers, you are limited to purchasing merchandise within that store. But these people are often well trained, hard working, and dedicated designers.

One reason for consulting a designer is that she will look at your home from an objective point of view. Some things that need changing, but to which you have become accustomed, will be apparent to an outsider. Another reason for consulting a designer is that professionals keep up to date on new products and know what works and what does not work. Many new products are short-lived and you don't want to be a home products guinea pig. A trained designer can be very helpful in assisting you in coordinating fabrics and colors, and in helping you find items that go with what you already have. A designer will advise you on carpets, hard-surface floor coverings, wall coverings, and upholstery fabrics and will help you in solving window problems.

Togetherness and privacy are both possible in the same area with thoughtful planning. The kitchen here can be open to the family room or hidden by folding doors. The dining room may be closed off for privacy or opened to permit use of one large area. *Courtesy of Pella Intermountain.*

Sometimes just getting approval of your own ideas from a professional is all you need to give you the confidence to proceed. But, in all fairness, have the courtesy and the good judgment not to pick the brains of a consulting designer and then go elsewhere to make your purchases.

On the other hand, why not be your own decorator? *You can be!* And if you study, ask questions, and take your time, it will be a most rewarding experience.

Have a plan, take your time, and don't compromise. A small economy is less important than the total effect of your house. If you can't afford what you really want, make a temporary substitution and wait to get the right thing when you can. This way, you will enjoy each purchase and there is a better chance of its being the right one.

As you study to acquire confidence in your ability to be your own decorator, inquire of good department stores, furniture stores, and design studios in your area about adult classes. Many of these institutions conduct decorating seminars either free or for a small fee. Such programs are usually presented by well-trained professionals who will not only cover the fundamentals of home decorating but also will acquaint you with the new materials that are available.

Most communities today have adult evening classes through the schools that can be very informative. Inquire at your local high school, college, or university. If they do not offer a course in interior design, chances are they will set up a survey at your request; and if enough people respond, the course will carry. This practice is going on in many communities across the country.

In some areas, there are now television courses in interior design that may be taken for credit or just for personal development. This may be only the beginning of a trend that could well become nation wide to meet the expanding demand by people who want help in improving their home environments.

4 Space -- Where There Is None

Probably the single most pressing problem of our time is space. People need space for togetherness; but equally as important, they need space for individual privacy. Wanting space for privacy is not just a personal whim. There is some evidence that persistent crowding from an early age can be harmful to the sense of individuality, an important feeling that can be fostered best in an atmosphere of privacy.

Besides space for togetherness and privacy, human beings need space for work, space for play, and space for doing the tasks of everyday living. They also need space for their things: big spaces, little spaces, open spaces, and closed spaces. They need space in which to carry out the daily activities that are essential to a productive life. But with skyrocketing prices, this vital commodity is becoming less and less available.

Space needs for families do not remain constant. As children grow from toddlers to teens, their needs change. As families expand and grow up, the need for more space may become critical. If building on to your present home or buying a larger place is financially out of the question, what, then, is the answer?

The satisfaction we get from space often has little to do with the actual measurements. The important thing is how that space is planned and controlled. We control our exterior space by the use of fences, walls, and hedges. We define interior space with partitions of various kinds; and within these areas, by the use of color, pattern, and furniture. Through the skillful use of scale, optical illusion, and other decorating tricks, the possibilities of visually expanding space are limitless.

A Search for Available Space

Before considering ways to expand space visually, look to the real space you already have. You may be amazed at the space not being used, or not to best ad-

An attic hideaway can provide cozy space for television viewing, reading, and relaxing. Heavy wood trim, deep blue walls, and a reddish brown rug form an appropriate background for a salamander side chair and the armoire that set the country French mood. ***Courtesy of Drexel Heritage Furnishings.***

vantage. And making better use of what you have is the most economical way to get space. Make a thorough survey of every inch of your house. Space can often be found in the most unexpected places. The first place to look is *up*. Do you have an attic? If the answer is yes, you have a practical opportunity to acquire good living space at relatively little cost. The angular shell that is already there can be an asset with great potential, and if you handle it skillfully, with inventive planning, you can work wonders. But be realistic! Check the strength of the floor; it may need bracing. When you lay flooring, it is usually wise to use lightweight flooring materials. If the ceiling is too low, there is a remarkable technique for raising it. Skylights and dormers provide light and air.

Next, look to the garage. If yours is like many others, it has become such a junk collector that there no longer is room for the car. With a minimum of construction work, that garage can be made into a spacious family room and/or recreation center. Its easy access to the outside makes it a natural for young people and their friends.

If you have a back porch, why not close it in to provide year-round living? Basements also have great potential. Because they muffle noise, basements accommodate activities without disturbing others.

If your living room feels too small and you find that pushing out walls is impractical, try removing the ceiling—literally! This can be done rather economically. Immediately the room opens up, taking on a new dimension. Even though floor space remains the same, the feeling of spaciousness will astonish you. Stain or repaint the rafters and ceiling joists. If you need more light, install a skylight.

Space for Your Things

Perhaps the problem that causes the most daily frustration in our homes is finding a place to put our things. Let's face it: most Americans are packrats. We don't need to apologize for it; we are all happier with our "things" around us. The only things that most of us are willing to throw away or send to the Goodwill Store are those belonging to other household members. We love our "junk," and we are offended when someone else calls it that. The only problem is that we just don't have room for it all. Things have a way of multiplying faster than space.

But it isn't only the personal things that are troublesome. There are all the necessary things that families accumulate. Things that are used only periodically or during certain seasons.

In a survey of scores of American families, *House and Garden* found that the most exasperating things to store were: "out-of-season clothing, the vacuum cleaner, garden equipment, out-door furniture, toys, bicycles, luggage, card tables, movie screens and projectors, and Christmas decorations." What can you do to make space for all of these things?

Start with Closets

Another key to easier living is well-planned storage space. But, you say, you don't have enough closet space. Is the problem really lack of closet space or lack of *organized* closet space? Experiment with one of your bedroom closets. First, take everything out of it and look it over. Often the area behind the wall on ei-

Order out of chaos.

ther side of the single door is not being used. Try this—remove the partition on the room side to expose the full space. Measure the space. Next list all the items to be hung, put in drawers, on shelves, or in boxes, and determine the space needed for each. Now subdivide the existing space. A shallow, unfinished chest of drawers may be a good starter. Leave space on one side for full-length items. On the other side, hang two rods, one above the other for waist-length clothes. Build full-length shelves above. Frame the opening and hang stock bifold doors. You will be delighted with the space you have literally made where there seemed to be none. It will hold twice what it did before, and items will be easier to find.

Check each closet in your house and repeat the same procedure, varying the organization of space to fit the particular need. Don't overlook the usable space on doors. Hanging shelves, shallow storage units, and pegboard can be attached to provide storage.

Try making a pair of closets. Using particle board, simply enclose about three feet of space on either side of your bed. Add doors, either louvered or with open panels designed to be hung with fabric. (Use the same fabric as your drapery or bedspread.) For a very little effort and at the loss of very little space, you will have gained two closets and added glamor to your room as well.

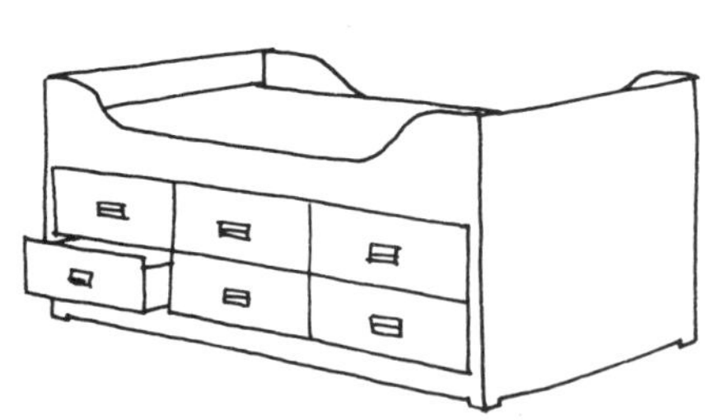

Underbed space can be valuable storage.

A carefully planned storage wall can hold innumerable things, both hidden and displayed. The television, conveniently placed, can be obscured behind a hinged panel when not in use. *Courtesy of Armstrong Cork Co.*

Space for the Television Set

A common problem in rooms with limited space is where to house the stereo and television. The answer again may be organization. Plan a complete entertainment center. Measure the available space. Then sketch a plan with compartments for each large item, such as the television. Use the remaining space for shelves to hold books and other objects. Use side-mounting metal shelf strips for flexibility. Base cabinets may be closed in to house necessary but sometimes unsightly objects. Stock cabinet doors are ideal, or the do-it-yourselfer may prefer to make them. For more limited space and a tight budget, a tension pole unit may be adequate. Versatile storage systems are available for almost any space and in a wide variety of styles and prices.

Making room for an entertainment center may require a rearrangement of the furniture. But the result can well be a more attractive and livable room.

What could be simpler, more versatile, or more attractive than these wicker collectibles? They belong in any home and in any room to conceal and organize any number of things. *Courtesy of Armstrong Cork Co.*

Storage for Little Things

If one key to easier living is *well-planned* storage space, another is storage space *where you need it.* Storage, conveniently located, not only simplifies your job of maintaining a reasonably neat house, but encourages neatness among household members.

Parts of games have a way of disappearing. Keeping track of the basic materials seems to be no problem, but a few necessary pieces are always lost. So, have a small chest, box, or foot locker in a central location, where lost articles can be tossed to be retrieved when needed.

Has it ever occurred to you that between the studs of room partitions there is unused space? The space isn't very deep, but it can hold a lot of small items. Studs are usually about sixteen inches apart. With a little skill, you can locate these by tapping the wall, but it is probably safer to use a simple, little gadget made especially for this purpose; probably you can borrow one. When you have located two studs, take out the wall in between and on the side where you want the storage. Paint the inside or line it with vinyl or vinyl-coated paper. Put in shelves, floor to ceiling if you wish, and "presto," you have an 8' × 16" × 4" storage—and you didn't lose an inch of floor space.

Enough Kitchen Space

How about your kitchen? Is there adequate space and storage there? Take a good look at your shelves and drawers. Perhaps you could manage just as well with more shallow shelves and drawers. Check what you put in them. There may be as much as a third of the

If hanging, well-polished cooking utensils please you, make a place for them. Also use every available niche for convenient storage. Warm fluorescent light will enhance your metals, colors, and wood grains. *Courtesy of General Electric.*

space wasted, which means that you can have a third more shelves and drawers.

Are the insides of your cupboard shelves used to their maximum? Doors can be equipped with shallow shelves. The wall space, usually eighteen inches, between the counter and cupboard is often not used. This is ample space for a shelf to hold spices or recipe books without interfering with counter space. Or, enclose this space to conceal small appliances.

Do you need a place for quick snacks in your kitchen? Look around. Maybe you could add a hinged drop-leaf counter to a storage unit; the counter could be lifted easily and supported by snap-up brackets. Another solution would be to insert a slide-out shelf below a counter top. This could double for quick snacks and a cutting board. If you have a section of unused wall, put it to work. Make a drop-leaf table of one leaf that can drop down when not in use.

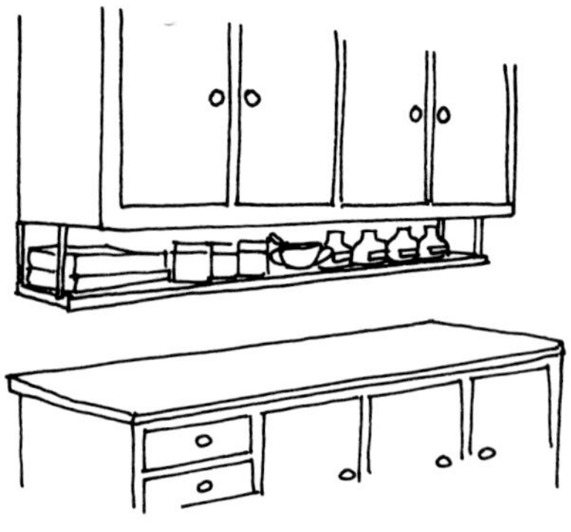

Add a shelf.

Left: A slide-out shelf provides work room. *Right*: A hinged dropleaf becomes an eating counter.

Special slots for often-used platters and trays and seldom-used appliances make use of the neglected "upper" part of the kitchen. Decorative baskets and herbs left for drying are attractively displayed. ***Courtesy of Armstrong Cork Co.***

How do you store your linens? Are they tucked away so that you have to press them every time you use them? There is a simple solution. Remove one or two bottom shelves from your linen closet and attach a board on each side slightly slanted to the front. Make round grooves for 1½ inch wooden cross-bars made from an old broom or dust mop handle. Sand the cross-bars, but do not paint them or the linen will slip off. Linen will be easily accessible and will stay unwrinkled.

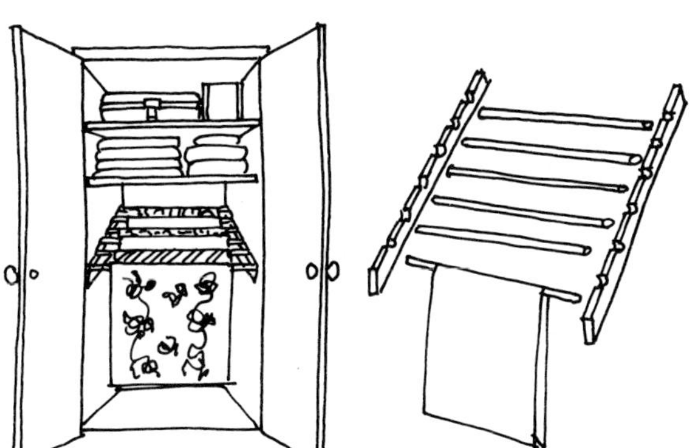

A simple solution for storing and keeping linens smooth.

Storage Space Just Anywhere

Look to unused wall space in any room where high shallow storage and display units may be added. A handy stepping stool itself, with a hinged door so it doubles as extra storage, makes reaching top shelves easy.

Space under stairways, often unused except as a receptacle for odds and ends that no one can find, can be converted into a half-bath, a laundry area, a telephone booth, a darkroom, or any one of a dozen or more useful purposes.

You have a garage, but there is no available storage space there—not even for the car! This is where you are really challenged to organize clutter. Attack first the little things: these are easiest to dispose of. The simplest and cheapest solution here is to cover an entire wall with pegboard. Purchase a generous supply of hooks of various sizes and hang up everything that can be securely supported; everything from hand snippers to folding patio furniture.

Where there is available space, build shelves or hang unfinished ones, or do-it-yourself cupboards. Insecticides, fertilizers, and other unsafe items should be put in high cupboards that can be locked. If space permits, floor-to-ceiling storage closets can hide and organize unlimited articles.

What to do with bicycles, skateboards, scooters, wheelbarrows, fireplace wood, and garbage cans is a perennial problem. Just fence them in—on three sides that is! Near the back door build an enclosure with the open side easily accessible but in the least conspicuous location. Outside, on the wall, plant vines and shrubs; inside, let the clutter accumulate.

***Left*: A wall of pegboard is a marvelous organizer. *Right*: Fence in unnecessary clutter.**

The correct placement of furniture can set aside an area of privacy and personal comfort. A well-planned storage wall provides good living and beauty. *Courtesy of Drexel Heritage Furnishings.*

Personal Space

In your search for space, don't forget to set aside an area for quiet relaxation. Tempers soon wear thin where there is no retreat from togetherness. Everyone needs a getaway room or a personal nook. Everyone needs, each day, a time to be alone and free from interruptions. This is especially important for the full-time homemaker. What the person *does* during this retreat is not important, but that he or she *has* this time is of major importance. It may be a time in which to put things into perspective or search for a solution to a pressing problem. It may be a time to do a bit of soul searching, or simply a time to relax and dream. But have some personal time *you must,* to carry on the responsibilities of daily living with a sense of confidence and well-being.

5

Taste - That Elusive Necessity

In the course of a lifetime, every homemaker will be required to use his or her creative abilities in planning a home environment. Window treatments, furniture arrangements, picture and memorabilia displays, floral arrangements, and table settings—all will reflect personal likes and dislikes. Because our physical environment has such a subtle but powerful influence upon our lives, we should take care in designing and arranging our daily surroundings in the best possible manner. When people live in well-proportioned, artfully decorated homes, they acquire an unconscious sense of what is good taste; and things that are overdone seem awkward, showy, and unpleasant to them. If good design is an integral part of our early environment, it becomes the right and natural thing throughout our lives. We live today surrounded by so much luxury that too often we lose sight of the importance of the little things that so often can make the difference between a house and a home. We derive great comfort and reassurance from seeing familiar things, such as the same rooms, furniture, paintings, books, and personal belongings. Through our day-to-day observations of these, values and attitudes are established in our lives.

One is not born with good taste, but it can be developed if one has the desire and is willing to work at it. Good taste is not acquired by thoughtlessly accepting each new fad. Fashion is not a good criterion of design. As with clothes, fashion in home furnishings may be good or bad design and may soon be outdated. It is important, therefore, that you learn to be discriminating in your purchases. Whether you are buying a crystal goblet, a chair, or a house, keep in mind that good taste is not determined by cost. Ultimately, taste is a sense of what is appropriate to your way of life. By surrounding yourself with things suitable to your pattern of living, you express your own taste. The success

Through the skillful use of line and texture, a sophisticated contemporary atmosphere is established. The vertical and diagonal lines in the wall, and the horizontal lines of the window shade are offset by the curved lines of the furniture and accessories. There is just enough smooth texture to relieve the rough surfaces. *Courtesy of Syroco.*

of your decorating depends not upon the expense or the elaborateness of the design involved, but upon the way you blend the ingredients that have been chosen with your home and needs in mind.

Good Taste Can Be Acquired

Through a deliberate and continuing process of first becoming "aware" and then training the eye to discriminate between good and bad design, good taste can be acquired. It is a matter of weighing, sifting, and considering.

First of all, acquire a knowledge of basic design principles, and then deliberately apply these principles until they become part of your decorating consciousness—until design that has been recognized over the years as "good" becomes good to you.

Develop the habit of careful and constant observation. Wherever you go, notice light and shadow, shape and texture, pattern, and color—not just a color in itself, but what colors do to each other. Look for balance, scale and proportion, rhythm, and emphasis. See and feel these in nature and sense the harmony they produce.

Become knowledgeable about interiors of historical and contemporary styles through study and research, by regularly examining periodical magazines, and by visiting furniture stores and decorating studios. Ask questions. Look, look, and look again. Study the principles and elements of design until you see how they can work for you.

Learn about accessories. Become knowledgeable about the small items appropriate for each style of furniture, and learn how you can use these to enhance rooms.

Design Principles—Defined and Applied

To develop good taste, one must first learn to discriminate between good and bad design. And the first step in that direction is to become familiar with the principles of design.

The principles of design are: proportion and scale, balance, rhythm, emphasis, and harmony.

Proportion and Scale

Proportion encompasses both the relationship of one part of an object to the other parts or to the whole and the relationship of one object to another, both aspects involving shape. It was the Greeks who found

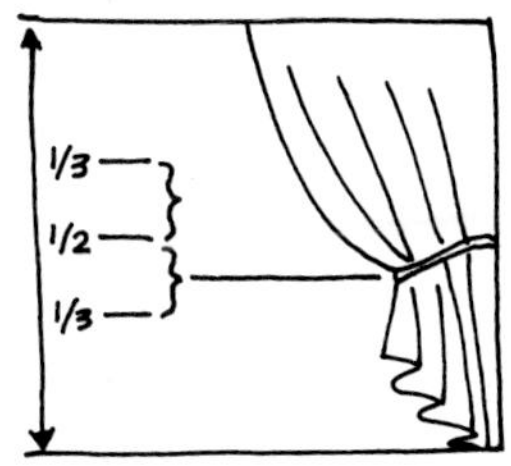

***Left*: Application of the proportions 4:7. *Right*: Application of the golden mean.**

that the square was the least pleasant proportion for an enclosure and that a rectangle was much better. Their standard for good proportion is a rectangle or oblong with its sides in a ratio of two parts to three. Called the *golden rectangle,* this standard is still honored today.

Other pleasant space relationships are 3 to 5, 4 to 7, or 5 to 8, and by multiplying any of these combinations of figures you can plan larger areas with similar relationships. Apply these proportions when planning the dimensions of a room or selecting a piece of furniture for a particular area. For example, if the living room side of your houses measures twenty-five feet, a desirable width would be fifteen feet. This is determined by multiplying 3' × 5' by five. (3' × 5' × 5 = 15' × 25'). If you have a seven-foot wall space against which to place a piece of furniture, the best size would be one which measures four feet in length. This would have the desirable ratio of 4 to 7.

The Greeks discovered, too, that the division of a line somewhere between one-half and one-third its length is the most pleasing. This *golden mean* should become part of your decorating consciousness. Apply this when planning any wall composition, such as the height for a mantel, for tying back drapery, or for hanging pictures, mirrors, or wall sconces.

The Greeks also discovered that odd numbers are more pleasing than even ones—that a group of 3 objects to 3 is more pleasing than 2 to 2 or 4 to 4, and that 2 to 3 is better than 2 to 4. Remember this also when creating wall compositions.

Scale refers to the overall size of an object or its parts as compared with other objects, regardless of shape. There is nothing more important to the success of a house and its furnishings than the correct use of scale and proportion. But because it is more a matter of taste than of mathematical correctness, weight and

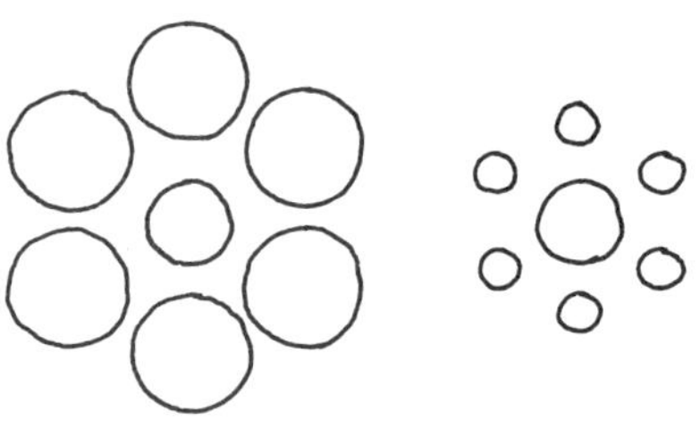

The central circles are identical. The apparent difference in size is caused by the difference in size of the surrounding circles.

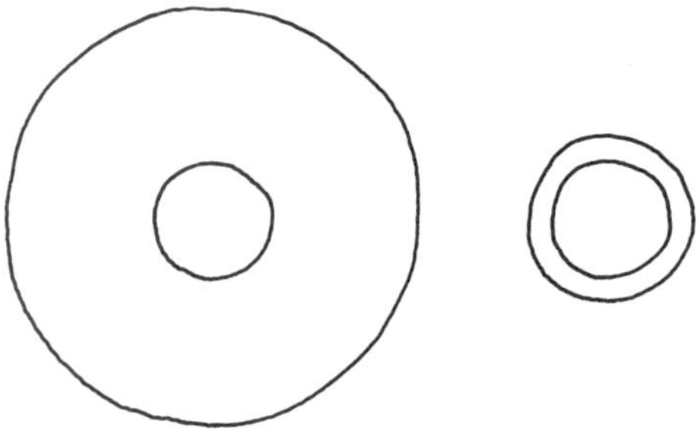

The central circles are identical. The apparent difference is caused by the difference in size of the surrounding area.

measurement will not always produce a feeling of rightness. For example, two love seats may have identical overall dimensions yet not look the same or be right together because one has heavier arms and shorter legs than the other.

Good scale and proportion must begin with the choice of the house on the lot and continue until the last accessory is chosen and put into place. We perceive an object in relation to the area around it. Objects that are too large will crowd a small room, making it appear smaller; in a large room, furniture that is too small will seem even smaller. Also, a large piece of furniture surrounded by small-scaled furniture will appear larger than when surrounded by large-scaled

Shade too small   Shade too large   Well scaled

Left*: Rhythm is an important component of every room composition. In this room *repetition* is seen in the use of the same fabric on the chair and the ottoman. *Gradation* is evident in the hanging of the ceiling lights. *Opposition* is clear in the right angles of the fireplace. *Transition* is shown in the round table, wicker shades, and lamp shades. *Radiation* is seen in the plants. *Courtesy of Armstrong Cork Co.

pieces. A small table with spindly legs placed at the end of a heavy sofa or chair will look out of place, while a large-scaled table placed near a dainty chair will not be pleasing.

Accessories such as mirrors, pictures, and lamps must be scaled for the items with which they are to be used. A lamp must not be overpowering for a table, nor should it be so small that it looks ridiculous. The lampshade must be the correct scale for the base.

Not only form, but color, texture, and pattern are important in the consideration of scale and proportion. Coarse texture, large patterns, and bold colors will cause the object on which they are used to appear larger than will smooth textures, small patterns, and soft, light colors. Keep in mind that the thing that attracts the eye seems larger. Through the skillful use of these and other principles, the apparent size and proportion of rooms and objects may be altered.

Balance

Balance is that quality in a room that gives a sense of equilibrium and repose. It is a sense of weight as the eye perceives it. There are three types of balance: formal, informal, and radial.

- *Formal* or *bisymmetric* balance is that in which identical objects are arranged similarly on each side of an imaginary line. Every room needs some bisymmetry, but too much becomes monotonous.
- *Informal, asymmetrical* balance is more subtle than bisymmetrical. It requires more thought and imagination, but, once achieved, it remains interesting for a longer time. In this type of balance, objects of different sizes, shapes, and colors may be used in an infinite number of ways. Two small objects may balance one large one; a small shiny object may balance a larger dull one; a spot of bright color may balance a large area of neutral. A large object moved closer to a central point will balance a smaller one pushed farther away. There is no measurement to tell you at what point to place these different sized items. The point at which balance is achieved must be sensed.
- *Radial* balance is balance in which all the elements of the design radiate from a central point. This is most often seen in a room where chairs surround a round dining table or a coffee table.

Most rooms need both formal and informal balance. Radial balance, which requires more space, is less often used.

Rhythm

Rhythm is an intangible component of a composition that helps the eye move easily about the room. It is achieved through the following techniques:

Repetition is achieved by repeating color, pattern, texture, line, or form as in a pair of lamps or by using the same fabric at windows and on furniture. *Gradation* is accomplished by varying the size of related objects from large to small or the color from dark to light. *Opposition* is produced wherever lines come together at right angles, as in the corners of a square window frame. *Transition* is found in a curved line, such as an arched window, drapery swags, or a circular chair. *Radiation* results when lines extend outward from a central axis, as in a lighting fixture or a bouquet of flowers.

Balance

Bisymmetrical

Asymmetrical

Radial

Compatible textures combine to create a room of comfort and warmth. The mellow barnwood paneling is an excellent foil for soft leather or vinyl. The large contemporary print, the slate floor, and the deep shag rug all contribute to a unified room with contemporary mood. *Courtesy of Henredon Furniture Industries, Inc.*

The fireplace is the focal point.

The large picture window is the focal point.

Emphasis

Emphasis in a room refers to the focal point or center of interest. In every well-planned room, there should be one feature toward which the eye is repeatedly drawn. It is this emphasis or focal point that can bring a feeling of order and unity into a room, and all other groupings should be subordinated to it. In most living rooms the focal point is the fireplace, a natural site for a main seating arrangement. Where there is no fireplace, a dominant architectural feature can be emphasized, such as a wall of books or a beautiful window. When an architectural point of interest is lacking, one must be created by some decorative means. A well-displayed art collection, a striking mural, a handsome and important piece of furniture, or a colorful rug are only some of the items that may become the dominant point in a room.

In creating, emphasizing, and enhancing a point of interest, you will be assisted by *color* (probably the most important element here) used artfully to achieve just the right amount of emphasis; *furniture* comfortably placed to focus on the point of emphasis but with a convenient opening so that the relationship to the rest of the room is an inviting one; *lighting* used to tie a group together or to create a dramatic effect; and *accessories* chosen with discrmination and artistically arranged to give importance and individuality to a grouping.

Harmony or Unity

Any well-designed room must have a unifying theme—one running through all the component parts and blending them together. The furnishings of a room should be in harmony with the background. For example, molded plastic chairs do not belong against formal eighteenth-century paneling, nor is a classic Louis XVI chair pleasing against a heavy black wall. Occasionally a surprising juxtaposition of seemingly unrelated objects may add relief, but this requires rather sophisticated judgment.

Furniture in the room should seem to "belong." It should be properly scaled and should reflect the feeling of the architectural background. *Colors* and *fabrics* must be appropriate for the style of furnishings. *Windows* must be treated to suit the mood of the room. *Floor coverings* should be selected with style and purpose in mind.

Harmony is best achieved by carrying out a basic theme or style. But never follow a style slavishly; rather, strive to maintain a general feeling of unity throughout, whether it be one of formality, casual elegance, or an informal country atmosphere. Within this overall theme, one may achieve individuality by an occasional surprise to give variety.

Elements of Design

Seven elements of design: texture, pattern, line, form, space, color, and light make up the components of a room.

Texture

Texture refers to the surface quality of objects, not only those qualities which are perceptible through the sense of touch, but those which have a clearly tactile quality; for example, the roughness of sandstone, the softness of a deep pile rug, and the smootheness of glass. Texture adds much visual interest to the environment, and modern interiors particularly depend upon it for variety and interest. The dominant texture of a room is usually established by the architectural background and should be carried out in the furnishings. For example, a room paneled in fine-grained, polished wood will require furniture and fabrics with smoother texture than a room paneled in natural barn wood.

Below Left: **Line is an important element in every room. Here is a good balance of vertical, horizontal, and curved. A stripe is coordinated with a floral wallpaper through the use of the same colors.** ***Courtesy of Imperial Wallcoverings. Below*****: A lighted soffit is an efficient means of lighting a person at the mirror and for general room lighting.** ***Courtesy of General Electric.***

Pattern

Pattern is created through the total arrangement of a room. The most obvious pattern is seen in fabrics, rugs, and wall coverings. Too much pattern can make a room too busy and uncomfortable, while a room that is devoid of pattern may be stark, dull, and lacking in character.

Line

Line establishes the feeling of a room, giving it a sense of motion or repose, and it may seemingly alter its proportions. Each kind of line has its particular psychological effect upon a room: *Vertical* lines tend to give height, strength, and dignity as seen in high furniture pieces and long straight drapery folds. *Horizontal* lines give a feeling of repose, solidity, and masculinity as seen in low, straight-lined furniture and bookshelves. *Diagonal* lines give a feeling of action and are evident in slanting ceilings and stairways. *Curved* lines have a gracefully feminine effect upon a room and are found in such things as archways, curved furniture, and drapery swags. Too much line movement in a room tends toward instability. Furniture should be static, and

Line

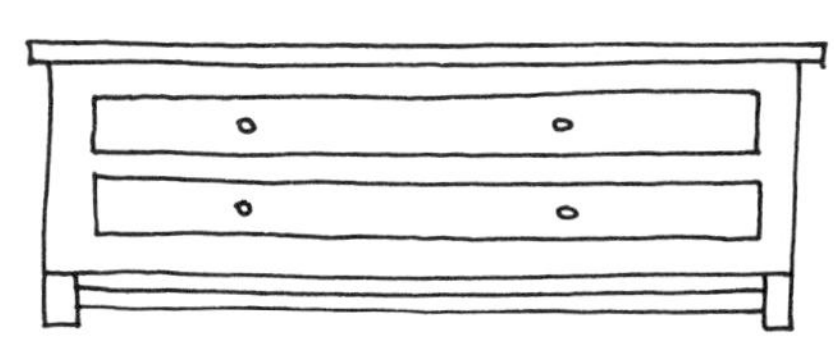

Horizontal

Vertical

Curved

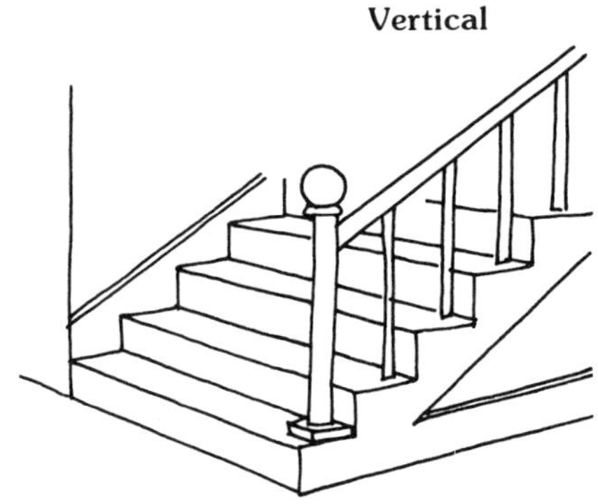

Diagonal

Below: A room with insufficient lighting. *Right*: The same room with warm white fluorescent tubes concealed behind a cornice board which reflects and provides general lighting to harmonize with light from portable lamps. *Courtesy of General Electric.*

curves should be restrained because a room completely decorated in curved lines is tiresome. Too many horizontal lines may become overpowering. A careful balance of line is essential to the ultimate success of a room's feeling of comfort and harmony.

Form

Form within a room is represented primarily in the furniture, the arrangement of which is discussed in chapter 12.

Space

Space is probably the most important element of domestic architecture. The arrangement of space is discussed in chapter 3.

Color

Color, that powerful decorating element, is discussed in chapter 6.

Light

Light is an indispensable element and, when skillfully used, can cover a multitude of decorating sins. Too little light, poorly balanced light, and poorly designed lamps and lighting fixtures can destroy an otherwise well-planned room. Lighting is also an important aspect of space. Our visual comfort and general mood are influenced by the *source, amount,* and *quality* of illumination. Every home should have both high and low levels of light, each depending upon its purpose. For particular mood and a touch of drama, new dimming controls can produce varying degrees of light. Up-to-date knowledge of lighting techniques, effects, and their integration with the other elements of the home is essential in good design.

There are many ways of decorating a house. But, your home should be decorated in your way, reflecting within the bounds of good taste, your personality, and should be suitable to your way of living. The knowledge and application of basic design principles and elements will help immeasurably in developing not only a sensitivity to good design, but a discriminating taste upon which to establish lasting values in creating beautiful and livable interiors.

6

Color--A Decorator's Best Friend

Although color is the most important and least expensive decorating tool, few people use it to the best advantage. Everyone knows that the primary colors are red, yellow, and blue, and that from these all other colors are made. They know what the standard color wheel is, but few people realize how much it can assist them in planning color schemes. Nor do they realize the miracles that can be wrought through the skillful use of color, such as altering the visual dimensions of a room and bringing balance into a room. For example, a long, narrow room can be made to appear shorter and wider when the two side walls are treated in a light, neutral color and the narrow end walls covered in a darker color or a bold pattern. This is a practical application of the simplest rule of color, which is that pale colors tend to recede and extend space, while brighter colors tend to advance and make an area appear smaller and more intimate.

It is common knowledge that people have definite color preferences. Each of us has a favorite color to which he or she is invariably attracted and with which he or she feels most comfortable. Because this is so, we should surround ourselves with colors that are pleasurable to us. Emotional reactions associated with color are spontaneous. But often the reaction is brought on by the *result* of a color rather than by the color itself, and the reaction may be positive or negative. "One such situation occurred in a meat market in Chicago, which, when painted a bright and cheerful yellow, lost business. A color consultant quickly informed the owner that the yellow walls caused a blue after-image, which gave meat a purplish cast, making it appear old and spoiled. The walls were repainted bluish-green, creating a red after-image that enhanced the appearance of meat—and sales zoomed." (John Dreyfuss, *Los Angeles Times*..)

Color, our most important decorating tool, is used dramatically here in strong contrast. The warm off-white sofa, set against a dark brown background with small bright accents, creates an elegant mood. *Courtesy of Hercules, Inc.*

Right: **The cool, monochromatic color scheme, using compatible textures and pattern, is suitable for a formal room. The delicate blues against white create a feeling of quiet elegance. *Fabrics by Stroheim and Romann. Photo by Stan Macbean. Lower right:* The warm, analagous color scheme is appropriate for an informal room. Colors are vibrant and closely related without being monotonous. *Fabrics by Isabella Scott. Photo by Stan Macbean.***

Conclusions drawn from this and other similar experiments, however, indicate a superficiality of information upon which, unfortunately, popular conclusions are based. Serious research on the subject is inconclusive and often contradictory, and there are frequently wide gaps between laboratory studies and their applications. Authorities in the field generally agree that color and emotion are closely related, and they agree that people react differently to color; but they are not in agreement upon the emotional effects of color, nor do they know why or whether these emotional reactions are inherent or learned.

Because we are constantly surrounded by colors, we tend to take them for granted, and often we do not really see them and so are unaware of their impact in our daily lives.

Color Clans Have a Mood

The simplest psychological division of color is into *warm* and *cool* colors. A line drawn between red and red violet and between green and yellow green on the color wheel will place warm colors on one side and cool on the other. When warm colors are intense, they are cheery, active, advancing, and somewhat informal, and they tend to blend objects together—a trait that can be applied to advantage when covering nondescript furniture pieces that you wish to make inconspicuous. However, warm colors used in strong intensity over large areas, such as a room with strong, red walls, may cause noticeable irritation. Such intense colors should be reserved for small accents in a room. Cool colors, particulary when used in tints, tend to be restful, soothing, receding, are somewhat formal, and make individual objects stand out, a trait that can be applied successfully when you wish to make a lovely object the center of focus. For example, put a turquoise velvet behind a gold vase. Beware of using too much cool color on large areas in some rooms; it tends to feel unfriendly and lack unity. An entrance way, for example, done in blue would lack the feeling of warmth and hospitality that you wish to establish there.

Colors falling midway between warm and cool, called *neutrals,* are of extreme importance in every color scheme. Large areas, such as walls and floors when done in warm neutral tones, tend to produce the most livable and lasting backgrounds. Cool neutrals can be successfully used, but are more difficult to work with.

Color's Three Characteristics

The three major characteristics of all colors are hue, value, and intensity or chroma. In order to understand color and how to use it successfully, one should become familiar with these terms.

Hue

Hue, or the color name, is that singular characteristic that sets each color apart from all others. A hue may be lightened, darkened, made more or less intense, but it will remain the same hue. In beginning a color

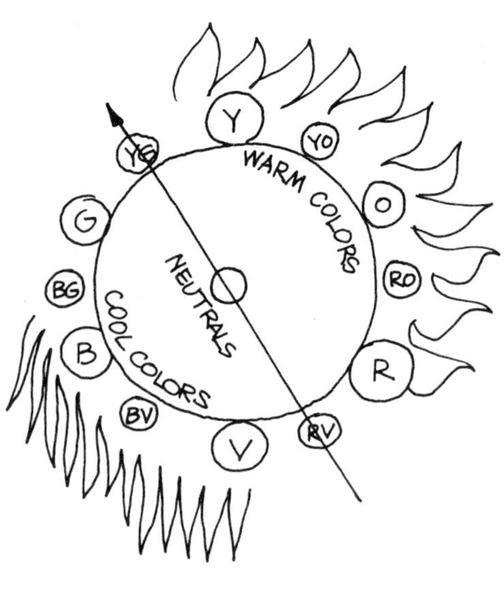

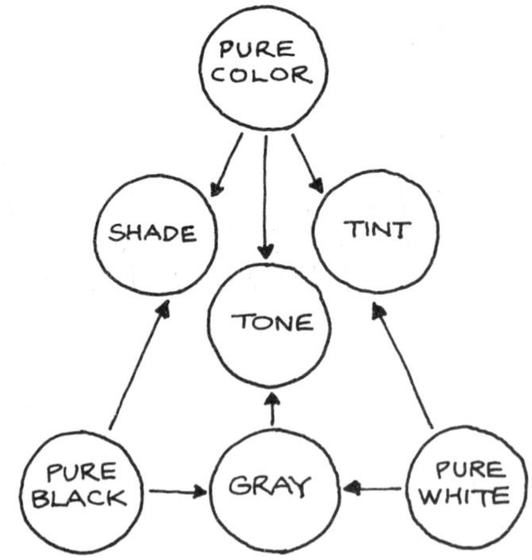

Black added to a color produces a *shade.* White added to a color produces a *tint.* When both black and white are added, the result is a *tone.*

scheme for any room, you should first choose one dominant color to serve as a starting point against which all other colors may be gauged. This color need not be repeated on all major pieces of furniture, but it should be repeated at least once to give a feeling of unity. The choice of color is a very personal one; but the size, proportion, function, style, and mood of the room, its exposure, and the amount of light in the room—all these must also be taken into consideration.

Value

Value is the degree of luminosity, the lightness or darkness, of a hue in relation to black and white. The value of any hue can be raised by adding white and lowered by adding black. When black or another darkening agent is added to a hue, the value is lowered and the result is a *shade* of that particular hue. When white is added to a hue, the value is raised and the result is a *tint*. Tints, either clear or neutralized, are most frequently used for large background areas such as walls and ceilings.

In addition to shades and tints, there is a third classification known as *tone*. A tone is formed by adding both black and white or a pigment of the color directly opposite from it on the standard color wheel. These grayed hues are extremely useful in working out colors where muted colors are necessary to "tone down" the brighter hues. Rooms are the most successful when they contain three tonal values: light, medium, and

Color can conceal and emphasize.

dark, with varying amounts of each. Allow large amounts of light to be set off by small areas of dark. Remember that a piece of furniture will appear larger if covered in a light fabric than a dark one. The use of sharp value contrast will also emphasize an object. For example, do you want to emphasize your front door, or do you wish to call attention to the fine lines of a dark piece of furniture? Then place the object against a light background. The dark will seem darker, and the light background will seem lighter. To make a piece of furniture unobtrusive, make it the same hue and value as the background. Black and white have a strong visible effect on other colors when brought into juxtaposition. Black tends to always make adjacent colors look richer. White reflects light into adjacent color. Often rooms which seem lifeless may be given sparkle and interest by the addition of black, white, or both.

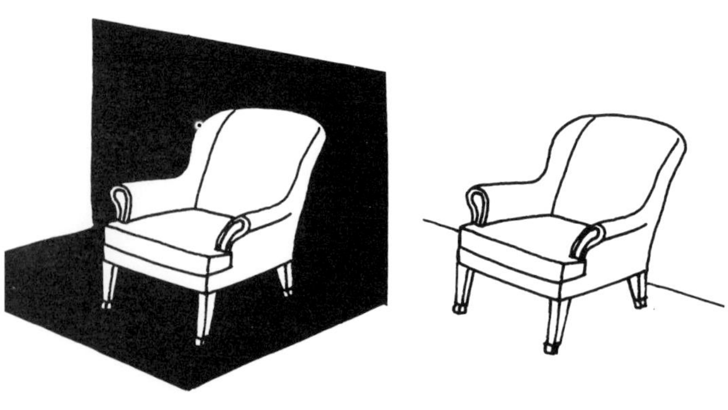

A light-value chair placed against a dark wall appears larger than against a light wall.

Intensity or Chroma

Intensity or chroma is the degree of saturation of pure color. As any color may be raised or lowered in value by the addition of white or black, so the *intensity* may be strengthened by the addition of pure chroma or *lessened* by the addition of that color's complement. The more of the color's complement that is added, the less pure color the original hue contains. The color has been neutralized.

A color may be made to appear more intense by placing it against its complementary color, a principle that has many practical applications. One is that a painting with predominantly orange hues will seem more orange if hung against a blue wall, but less orange when hung against a wall with warm browns—including some orange—tones.

When planning color schemes for your rooms, keep in mind that strong chroma is conspicuous and size-increasing; furniture will seem larger and will fill up a room more if intense colors are used. Walls in strong chroma will seem to advance and make the room appear smaller. Since rooms are backgrounds for people, colors should not be too demanding. It is wise, to choose colors in softly neutralized tones for large background areas in most rooms where people spend much time. Intense colors should be reserved for small

Walls in light color tend to recede.

Walls in strong chroma tend to advance.

areas and accents. This principle, called the *law of chromatic distribution*, is one of the safest guides in planning a color scheme: "*The large areas should be covered in the most neutralized colors of the scheme. As the areas reduce in size, the chromatic intensity may be proportionally increased.*" (Whiton, *Interior Design and Decoration.*) This principle of color distribution produces rooms with a feeling of serenity in which one may live comfortably for a long period of time.

Basic Color Schemes

In general, all color schemes fall into two categories; related and contrasting. Within these the variations are endless. Related colors produce harmonious schemes that may be cool, warm, or a combination of both. Contrasting schemes have great variety and tend to be more exciting, particularly if strong chroma is used. In any scheme, black or white or both may be added without changing the scheme.

There are three basic color schemes; and, although professional designers seldom select a specific one to begin with, the final scheme often falls into one of these categories; monochromatic and achromatic, analogous, and complementary.

Monochromatic and Achromatic

Monochromatic color schemes are developed from a single hue but with a range of values and different degrees of intensity. Unity is probably the most notable thing about this type of scheme; and, if light values predominate, space will be expanded. There is a danger that a one-color scheme may become monotonous; but, if one looks to nature where monotony is never present, the guidelines are clearly apparent. Examine the petals of a rose and use the shadings from soft delicate pink to deep red for a feminine bedroom. See the tones and tints of the green in a leaf and the variety of chroma in the brown bark of a tree. Try combining nature's colors in a room using the lighter, neutralized tones for large wall areas, slightly deeper tones for the carpet, medium tones for large furniture, and vivid chroma for accents.

Achromatic color schemes are those that possess no hue. They are made up entirely of black, gray, and white. Striking textures in fabrics, woods, metals, and glass are necessary to bring life and interest into the monochromatic and achromatic schemes. When done well, these color schemes present a sophisticated and often dramatic effect particularly appropriate for modern rooms.

Analogous

Analogous or related color schemes are produced from any segment of colors that are in juxtaposition but contain no more than half the colors on the standard color wheel. This color scheme has more interest, is more widely used, and is less difficult to achieve successfully than the monochromatic. Analogous color schemes are easy, natural, and comfortable to live with, and they may be warm, cool, or a combination of both.

Complementary

Complementary or contrasting color schemes are probably the most widely used of all the color schemes since they have more variety. These may be developed in a number of different ways, but each one uses colors of contrasting hues. Complementary schemes will always have some warm and some cool colors since they are opposite on the color wheel. These schemes are appropriate for either traditional or modern interiors. In strong chroma they are lively and vigorous, while in grayed tones they may be subtle and restful.

Other Methods of Creating Livable Color Schemes

In addition to the three basic color schemes, there are many other methods of developing livable color schemes.

- Start with your favorite color, or a color you wish to use for a particular room, and then find other colors that blend with it. If you are not sure of your own ability, see the helpful charts at your paint dealers.
- If you are a bit daring, select two or three bold colors you like and build around them or use white plus one color. This may sound elementary, but it may well produce the most beautiful and sophisticated room in your house.
- Start with a neutral background and play three or four harmonious colors against it (accented neutral).
- Copy a color scheme you like from a magazine or a room in a furniture store.
- Start with a lovely fabric, wallpaper, or rug. Follow the law of chromatic distribution by choosing one of the lightest, most neutral colors of the room's background and using the other colors on various objects in the room, reserving the most intense color for accents.

- Let a prized picture determine your color scheme. Follow the same procedures as with fabric. Whatever method you follow, the result should be a livable color scheme appropriate for the particular room for which it was planned and for the people who will live there.

The Effects of Adjacent Colors Upon Each Other

There is no more important fact to remember about color than this: *The eye perceives color not in and of itself, but in relation to its environment.* A color is not important in itself; the significant thing is what happens when different colors are brought together. Evidence of this is that when the eye sees a colored object, it induces that color's complement in the environment. For example, when a green chair is placed against a light neutral background, the eye sees a tinge of red in that background. When contrasting colors having strong chroma with the same value are used against each other, they will clash, producing a vibration that will be fatiguing. When contrasting colors with strong differences in value are used, side by side or one against the other, the colors will stand out but will not clash. For example, if a fabric has a purple ground and an orange pattern, and both are the same value and the same strong intensity, the pattern will vibrate and be distracting. But, if the orange pattern is a darker value than the background, it would neither clash nor vibrate.

The Effects of Natural and Artificial Light on Color

Without light there is no color; and light, both natural and artificial, is an important element in any room composition. Rugs look deeper, fabrics more luxurious, metals take on an exotic glow, woods become softer, and the mood may become dramatic, lively, or warm and intimate.

Natural Light

In planning your color scheme, remember that the natural light in the room will have a definite effect upon the colors. A room with a lot of natural light may be more pleasant with darker colors that absorb the light and reduce glare, and a room with less light may need light-reflecting colors. The direction from which the light enters the room also affects colors. Light from the north is cool; from the east it is more neutral; and from the south and west it is warm. Light also varies throughout the day.

Artificial Light

Artificial light has a very definite effect on colors depending upon the light source (incandescent or fluorescent), reflective traits of the surface materials, the level of illumination, and the method of lighting.

Light Source. The ordinary incandescent light casts a warm glow; the fluorescent tubes come in white, warm and cool tints. White light, the most natural, emphasizes cool colors. Warm light is the most flattering and is usually preferred where a soft, low level of illumination is desired. Warm light accentuates warm colors and neutralizes cool colors. Cool light intensifies cool colors and deadens warm colors. Warm light is friendly and tends to unify objects. Cool light expands space, produces a crisp atmosphere, and tends to make individual objects stand out.

Surface Materials. As with natural light, artificial light will be absorbed by dark colors and nubby textures and reflected by light colors and shiny surfaces.

Level of Illumination. The level of illumination or quantity of light will affect colors. We have all experienced the stimulating effect of color in a room when the light is very bright and the relaxing feel when light is low. So, colors may become dull, lifeless, and dreary with insufficient light. As illumination increases, colors become more vibrant.

Method of Lighting. With direct lighting the rays of light fall directly from the source onto the surface; with indirect lighting the light is directed upward and reflected from another surface, usually from the ceiling down onto the area to be lighted. An indirect light produces an effect resembling the light of midday. This is a practical method of lighting for kitchens and work areas, but it is the most unflattering light for living areas because it tends to give the feeling of flat monotony. When used alone, it may produce a commercial feeling. Portable lamps can give direct light, indirect light, or both, and with a diffused effect can produce soft shadows that alter colors, adding interest and charm to a room. They can light any area for any purpose, creating decorative effects in a unique way.

Artificial light, when understood and used with skill, may alter, subdue, highlight, or dramatize the colors of a room in a way that no other decorative medium can. Because there are so many variables, it is impossible

Timeless traditional. This eighteenth-century room is done in colors typical of the period. The Persian rug sets the color scheme. Paneled walls pull out the soft green. The red damask on the Chippendale style sofa and desk chair emphasizes the richness of the furnishings. *Courtesy of Henredon Furniture Industries, Inc.*

to set down definite rules in the use of light and color. Therefore, before you select a color for a specific setting, you should try it in that setting, observing it during different hours of the day and after dark.

Other Important Considerations in the Use of Color

- The effects of texture upon color. Color appears different when the texture is varied. Fabrics with a deep, textured surface such as pile carpet, velvet, and all manner of nubby weaves that cast tiny shadows will appear darker than a smooth fabric that is dyed with the same hue having the same value and chroma, because the smooth surfaces reflect the light. A rough textured wall may appear grayed or soiled under artificial light because of shadows cast from the uneven surface. A smooth, shiny surface will reflect light that can be well utilized. A dull or matte surface will absorb color; and, if it is dark as well, it may absorb all of the color.
- The effects of distance on color. Near colors appear more brilliant and darker than the same colors at a greater distance. Therefore, brighter and darker colors used in large rooms will seem less demanding than the same colors used in small rooms. Colors appear stronger in chroma when covering large areas. For example, a small color chip may be the exact color tone you feel you want for your room, but when that tone is painted on four walls, it looks much darker because the area of that color chip has been multiplied many thousands of times. When selecting a wall color from a small color chip, always choose one several tints lighter than you wish the completed room to appear. It is advisable to paint a sizable area of color on walls in opposite corners of the room and observe them in the light at different times of the day and night before making the complete application.
- The use of off-white. There is a common notion among many untrained individuals that off-white in itself is a specific color and goes with anything. This is far from the truth. Off-white is white tinted with a hue—any hue. But to be compatible, off-whites must contain only the same hue. For example, off-white walls, ceilings, glass curtains, and fabrics used in the same room, must be tinted with the same hue. Warm off-whites are more easily blended than cool off-whites.

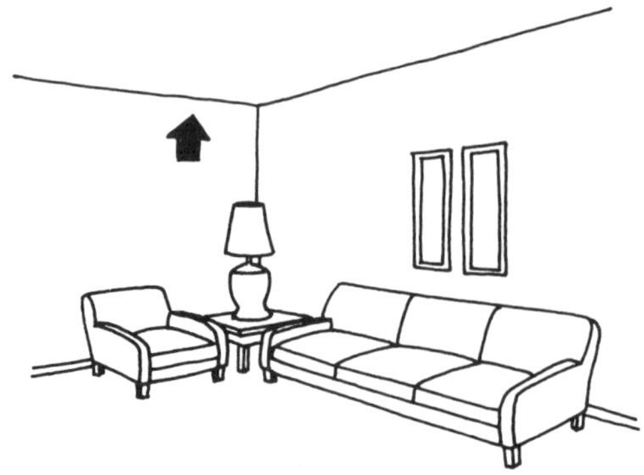

A light color makes a ceiling appear higher.

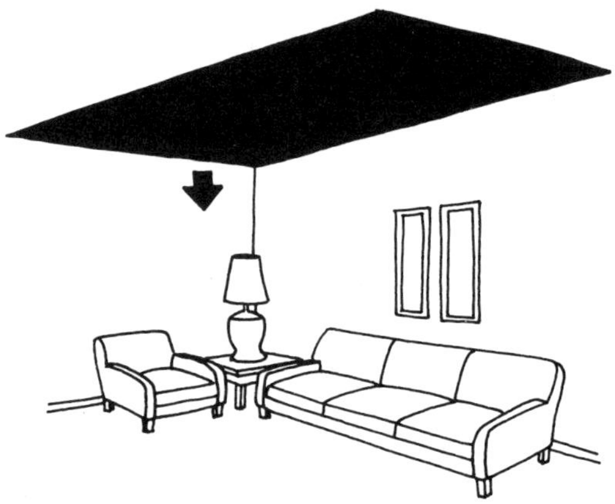

A dark color makes a ceiling appear lower.

- The use of color for wood trim. The color of the wood trim is important to the general color scheme of the room. When painted, it may be the same hue, value, and intensity as the wall; a darker shade of the wall hue; or a color that contrasts with the wall, if it is pleasantly related to some other major color in the room.
- The use of color on the ceiling. The ceiling is the largest unused area of a room, and its color is important to the general feeling. If the objective is to have the wall and ceiling look the same, the ceiling must be a tint of the wall, because the reflection from the walls and floor tends to make the ceiling look several shades darker than it actually is. If the walls are papered, the ceiling may be a tint of the background or the lightest color in the paper, preferably an off-white. If walls are paneled in dark wood, the ceiling is better painted a light tint of the wood color. If the wood trim is painted white, a white ceil-

Color can help set or add to the mood of a room. Here the bold colored stripe in the heavy texture is compatible with the rough plaster wall, the shag rug, and the wicker table, and adds just the right accent. Notice also the distribution of value: dark, light, and medium. *Courtesy of Hercules, Inc.*

ing is advisable. When the ceiling is too high, a dark shade will make it appear lower.

- The use of color when selecting drapery. The success of any room is largely dependent upon the treatment of the windows, and the color used in the drapery fabric may make the windows the room's most conspicuous element. If the objective is to have a completely blended background effect, choose drapery fabric that is the same hue, value, and intensity as the wall. If a contrasting effect is desirable, select a color that contrasts with the wall, but one which relates well with the other colors used throughout the room. Glass curtains are usually most pleasing when they are an off-white, blended to the drapery.
- The use of color when walls are paneled. Where dark wood paneling is used, colors of rather intense chroma should be used about the room since deep wood tones absorb color. If paneled walls are light, colors may be light, either blended or contrasted. If paneling is formal, colors should have a rich formal look. If paneling is informal, colors should have the same feeling.
- The use of color in altering the apparent size and proportion. The object that attracts the eye seems larger; therefore, items of furniture may be made to appear larger if painted or upholstered with colors having strong chroma. A small room may be made to feel even smaller if demanding colors, which are space filling, are used on backgrounds and furniture.

On the other hand, light, blended, and receding colors will expand a room and seem to create more space. Through the skillful use of color, a room's visual dimensions may be significantly altered.

- The use of color in bringing balance into a room. Because objects that attract the eye seem larger and therefore feel heavier, a small area of bright color will balance a large area of softly muted color, and a small area of dark color will balance a larger area of light color. For example, a small bouquet of bright flowers placed near one end of a long table will balance a rather large lamp of soft color placed near the other end. A small, dark blue plate on a shelf will balance a much larger white one.
- The use of color in transition from one room to another. Whenever two rooms adjoin, there should be a pleasant relationship of color and pattern. One or more colors should be carried from one room to the other but not necessarily used in the same manner. For example, the accent color in the wallpaper of an entrance hall may be neutralized and used on the walls of the adjoining living room or emphasized in a piece of upholstery fabric. When dining and living rooms are open, walls, drapery, and floor coverings should be the same or closely related. Whenever one room may be seen from another, there should be an easy transition of color to give a feeling of unity.
- The use of color in period rooms. Because particular styles and periods of furnishings have colors that reflect their character and set the feeling of authenticity, colors should be chosen with discrimination when decorating period rooms. Many excellent books provide full information on the subject.
- The use of color distribution. Color is the most unifying element available to the decorator, and its skillful distribution is essential to the feeling of harmony. Remember the importance of values, the law of chromatic distribution, and that each room needs one dominant color to which all others are subordinated.
- The effects of color upon the mood of a room. Color more than any other element is capable of setting the general mood of a room, and don't overlook the importance of wood as a color. Rich, muted tones produce a mood of tranquility, while lively, contrasting colors produce an informal mood. There are general color moods which seem appropriate for specific areas of the house. The *entrance hall* is the room that introduces people to your home. Whatever theme you have chosen for the major rooms, let your entrance way emphasize this. *Living areas* used for more formal purposes should generally have neutralized color schemes to produce an atmosphere of tranquility. More informal living areas, such as family and recreation rooms, need more lively color schemes to produce an informal atmosphere. *Dining rooms* are at their best when the color schemes are unobtrusive, thus permitting a variety of table decoration as well as a serene dining atmosphere. *Kitchens and other work areas* are usually more desirable when large areas of color are light, fresh, and clean-looking, with accents of strong chroma. *Bedrooms and bathrooms* are the private areas of the house, and personal preference should be the determining factor in the choice of colors.
- Color as a reflection of individual personality. Color provides unlimited opportunity for expressing individuality; let it express yours. If you choose, be bold and modern. Bold colors need not be garish. Use unusual combinations if they please you. If you prefer neutralized colors, use them; they need not be drab. Neutralized color schemes are more difficult to achieve than bright contrasting ones, but when accomplished, they have a lasting quality. When selecting colors, consider current trends, but don't let them be the determining factor. Regardless of what colors are in fashion, the individual's preference should always be the main consideration. The most important thing to remember in the use of color is that there are no absolutes at any time; and to achieve, through knowledgeable choice and distribution of color, beautiful and livable schemes for every room throughout the house is the greatest challenge to the decorator—and possibly the greatest reward.

7

Fabric -- The Miracle Worker

Visualizing the way a room can look complete with new wall covering, drapery, rugs, and upholstery is one of the most difficult things for the untrained person. So don't commit yourself to purchasing everything you need all at once. Get one thing at a time and live with it for a while. Each purchase will help you with the subsequent purchase. For example, suppose your initial plan was to paint the walls of your living room a rich, warm, off-white with blended drapery, a near-brown rug, and then have a sofa covered in a fabric containing mostly browns and orange. But, when the rug was down and the drapery hung, the room needed some lively contrast. So after trying several pieces of fabric, you decided on something quite different for the sofa. You chose a printed linen, predominantly blue. You hadn't considered blue before, but this introduced just the right contrast the room needed. Had you made the decision earlier, you would have made a different choice and one not so much to your liking. After living with the new sofa for a while, it would be easy to select accent colors for the room taken from the colors in the sofa. Don't be in a hurry to get everything at one time. Take your time and consider each purchase with care and discrimination.

Probably the single most important thing you will do in establishing the atmosphere or mood of your home is choosing the fabrics. Never trust your color memory. Always try samples in your own environment before making a selection.

Never has the choice of fabric been as great as it is today. New miracle fibers are woven in materials for every decorative purpose and are made to be lived with and enjoyed. As never before, today's homemaker may satisfy her idea for elegance and practicality at the same time. Yes—you can have your cake and eat it too!

The Importance of Knowing Fibers

Because of the abundance of fibers in today's textiles, the person shopping for fabrics may be overwhelmed when confronted with the complexity of fibers and textures. But with a little effort, the decorator can become familiar with the most common fibers, both natural and man made. Then, knowing what can be expected from each fiber, and recognizing the specific decorating problem at hand, he or she will make wise choices when selecting fabrics. Knowing the characteristics of the fibers affords answers to such important questions as: How will the fabric wear? Will it fade, stretch, or shrink? Will it hold up under heat? Will it launder well, or must it be dry cleaned? There was a time when with little training one could identify the fiber content of a fabric by the feel. But this is no longer so. Some man-made fibers have been developed to simulate the feel of natural fibers so closely that today one must rely upon government labels to determine the true fiber content.

Following are the most common fibers used today, both natural and man made; become familiar with the most common uses and characteristics of each and the generic names of the man-made fibers. This will help you become an informed and intelligent shopper.

Natural Fibers

Natural fibers commonly referred to as plant and animal are further classified as protein, cellulose, and mineral.

Protein Fibers

The protein fibers are wool, silk, and leather. Wool is probably the most important natural fiber. It contains most of the desirable qualities: it wears well, cleans well, resists dirt, is resilient, and is a good insulator. It can be woven fine or coarse, loose or tight, and can be dyed from the palest to the deepest colors. In recent years, its use has been limited because of cost.

Silk is the luxury fiber and yet is very strong. It takes and holds dyes well but does not hold up in direct sunlight. The cost makes it prohibitive to most people.

Leather, although not a fiber, is an animal product that has long been used for household purposes, both for utility and beauty. It is pliable, extremely durable, and may be used in natural color or dyed. Real leather is expensive but has been simulated to a remarkable degree by vinyls that have virtually replaced it, except in the most prestigious contracts.

Cellulose Fibers

Cellulose fibers consist of cotton, linen, and ramie. Cotton is a pleasure to work with because of its great versatility, its ability to take and hold colors, and the unlimited fabric types into which it can be made—everything from the simplest muslin to elegant damask. It is the most plentiful natural fiber.

Linen is strong and pliable, takes and holds colors, is absorbent, but wrinkles unless chemically treated—a process that reduces its durability. Linen is expensive. Ramie, or grass linen, resembles linen.

Man-Made Fibers and Their Uses

In addition to the natural fibers, there are a number of man-made fibers, each with its own generic name, such as nylon or rayon, that the Federal Trade Commission requires be put on the label of all textiles; so, if you know the general characteristics of each fiber family, you are in a position to choose the fabric that best suits your needs. However, the fiber alone will not insure good performance; dyes, weaves, and finishes that are not properly handled will reduce the quality of performance. Unfortunately, however, you will not always be able to judge these things. So you must rely upon the reputation of the manufacturer and the retail dealer. Nevertheless, being familiar with the characteristics of each generic group will help you greatly in making a selection.

Along with the generic name, you will also find a trade name. This is the manufacturer's label to identify his particular product. There are literally hundreds of trade names, making it almost impossible for the consumer to recognize them all. But being familiar with the more reliable trade names will help assure you of a quality purchase. Your guide in knowing what you are getting is the *generic label. Always read this before making a purchase.* It is your assurance of what you are getting. Once you have identified the generic name of the fiber, the following chart should help you select fabric for any household purpose.

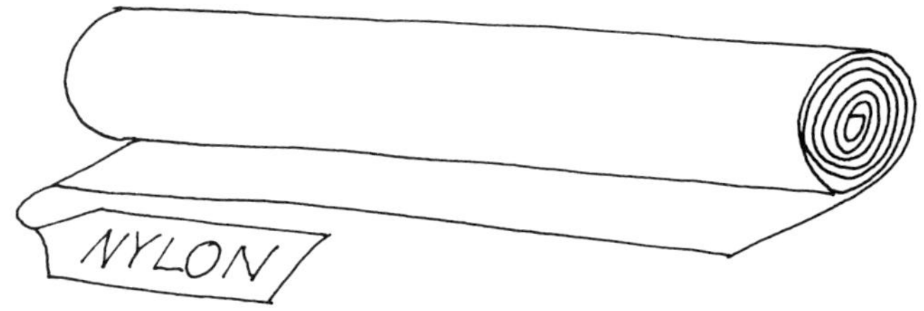

Always read the generic name on the label.

Most Common Made-Made Fabrics

Generic Name and Some Trade Names	Some Principal Uses	Major Characteristics	Care Instructions
Acetate Acels, Aviscos, Celanese, Estron,	Drapery, upholstery, bedspreads	Economical, drapes well, holds shape, nonfading	Dry cleaning recommened. Some can be washed in mild lukewarm suds. Press on wrong side with warm iron.
Rayon Bemberg, Aviscos, Fortison, Skyloft	Upholstery, drapery, bedspreads, slip covers	Highly absorbent, durable, soft, drapes well, creases easily, fair durability, moderately priced	Wash in lukewarm suds. Press on wrong side with warm iron.
Nylon Antron, Cadom Cumuleft, Tycors Nyler 6/6 and 66	Carpets, upholstery, slip covers, drapery, bedspreads	Exceptionally durable, holds shape, resists wrinkling and mildew, resilient, takes dye well, deteriorates in sun	Machine wash in warm water. Machine dry at low temperature. Use warm iron.
Acrylic Acrilan, Creslan Orlon, Zefron	Carpets, curtains, drapery, upholstery, slip covers, bedspreads shower curtains	Luxurious; resilient; quick drying; long wearing; does not shrink, sag, or stretch; dyeable in any color; mildew resistant	Machine wash. Use fabric softener. Machine dry. Use only warm iron.
Polyester Dacrons, Encron Fortrel, Kadel, Trivera	Carpets, upholstery, slip covers, drapery, curtains, bedspreads, shower curtains	Durable; resists wrinkles, mildew and sunlight, shrinking and stretching; dyes well; amenable to all constructions; resistant to chemicals	Machine wash in warm water with soap or detergent. Machine dry or drip dry.
Olefin Durel, Herculon, Marvess, Patlon, Polycrest, Vectra	Kitchen and outdoor carpets, upholstery	Lightweight; wears well; highly stain resistant; resistant to chemicals, mildew, and rot; quick drying; heat sensitive	Machine wash in lukewarm water. Use fabric softener. Blot carpet stains with absorbent tissue.
Glass fibers Fiberglas, Pittsburgh PPG	Curtains and drapery (beta fiber used for bedspreads)	Fireproof; impervious to moisture, mildew, sun and salt; will *not* stand friction; quick drying	Wash (machine washing not recommended)

The beautiful floral print sets the color scheme in this room. The soft green is used on the pair of chairs; the off-white, on the small lounge chair; and the drapery and rug are blended to the brown background. Country French is seen in the coffee table, the end table, and the painted commode and mirror on the landing. *Courtesy of Drexel Heritage Furnishings.*

What Goes with What?

Coordinating colors and fabrics in good taste is probably the number one problem in decorating. And how to do it is the question most often asked. Actually, there is no pat answer. Combining fabrics is a matter of training and skill. Some people seem to have an aptitude for acquiring this skill while for others it takes more patient study and practice. Although an unexpected combination of materials may create a feeling of great interest and charm, there are some general principles that should be helpful to the inexperienced when combining colors, textures, and pattern.

When the design in a fabric has motifs sufficiently large in scale, or with enough contrast in color or tone to permit the eye to clearly distinguish them, we say it has pattern. When the parts of the pattern are so subtle or are blended in such a way that they are indistinguishable, except at close range, it becomes more texture than pattern. Fabrics that make no pretext at pattern such as plain satin, taffeta, tweeds, and heavy

Poorly coordinated patterns.

A room without pattern may lack character.

basket weaves, are described as having texture only.

Many people are afraid of patterned fabrics and avoid them entirely. Others use them ineffectively. Although they are not a necessity, most rooms are enhanced by a well-chosen patterned fabric, and in skillful hands defects may be camouflaged, beauty and glamour added, and decorating miracles performed.

As with color, there are no absolute dos or don'ts regarding the use of pattern, but a few general guidelines may be helpful:

- Patterns used within the same room must have a pleasing relationship to each other. There should be common elements that tie them together to create a workable relationship. One or more of the elements, such as color, texture, or motif, running throughout will give an easy flow of unity to the entire scheme.
- The principal pattern need not be repeated in the room so long as one or more of the colors in that pattern are carried over into other areas. You may, however, with pleasing results, repeat the same pattern on several pieces of furniture, or use it at the windows and on the furniture, or on the walls, windows and furniture, depending upon the overall effect you desire. Odd pieces of furniture are unified when covered in the same fabric, and the repetition of the fabric will bring unity into an entire room. The pattern must be chosen with discrimination since the final product should not be too busy, too stimulating, or overpowering.
- With very few exceptions, a room will be more pleasant to live in for a long time if it has no more than one bold pattern of the same type of design, such as a floral. Once the dominant motif is established, it may be supplemented by a small pattern, a stripe, a check or plaid, and appropriate plain textures.
- When combining patterned fabrics, scale must be considered. Bold, informal patterns call for heavy textures and strong color combinations; refined formal patterns call for smooth textures and softer colors.

There are no positive dos or don'ts in combining fabrics, but if fabric know-how—which involves color, pattern, and texture—is combined with experience and skill, the result should be a pleasant one. Unusual juxtaposition of fabric may create a dramatic effect, but this kind of carefree sophistication usually develops from a knowledge and practice that has produced a

"Oh, Nancy, I'm home! Nancy, where are you?"

Fabric can set the mood of a room. *Below Left*: The informal blue-onion print sets the mood. The simple furniture and rag rug carry out the theme. *Courtesy of The Warner Co. Below*: The beautiful satin stripe, well coordinated with the floral print and the antique velvet used against the plain carpeting, creates a room of formal beauty. *Courtesy of Drexel Heritage Furnishings.*

certain self-confidence in daring to do the unexpected. To begin with, the novice would be wise to follow the basic guidelines.

Formal and Informal Fabrics

Fabrics fall into two general categories: formal and informal, although many are versatile enough to go almost anywhere.

Formal Fabrics

Formal fabrics are those with smooth texture, usually stylized patterns, and traditional stripes. Colors will likely be more neutralized. Some examples of formal materials are velvet, damask, brocade, brocatelle, satin, shantung, and taffeta. These fabrics are appropriately used in rooms with a period feeling such as Georgian, Eighteenth-century French, and formal contemporary.

Informal Fabrics

Informal fabrics are those with a rougher texture such as burlap, canvas, hopsacking, muslin, tweed, and boucle. Patterns may be bold, naturalistic, abstract, or geometric. Color will usually be stronger and contrastive. Fabrics that look handcrafted will come in this category. These fabrics are at home in rooms with a rustic or country look, such as Early American, Country French, and modern.

Many materials can be used in either category. For example, glazed chintz may have a stylized pattern and rich colors and may fit into a formal setting, or it may have a quaint pattern and lively colors that will make it at home in an English country or Early American room. Also, tapestry may go anywhere, depending upon the color and pattern.

Solving Decorating Problems with Fabrics

Problems that can be solved through the expert use of fabrics are unlimited. Listed below are some of the ways in which fabric may serve many purposes and may come to the rescue of the decorator if he or she is knowledgeable about its use. The correct fabric can

- Lighten or darken a room

Here the oriental rug is the starting point for coordinating fabrics. Colors from the rug are used throughout the room. The plain drapery, floral couch, and geometric patterns on chair and ottoman all draw from the rug colors, creating a pleasing combination. ***Courtesy of Hercules, Inc.***

- Hide unsightly features, such as an old-fashioned radiator.
- Emphasize or conceal windows, walls, or furniture.
- Set the mood of a room; give it a feeling of formality by the use of stylistic design, smooth weave, and rich colors—or of informality by the use of naturalistic or abstract designs, textured weaves, and bold color.
- Bring harmony and unity into a room by repeated use of the same fabric.
- Bring balance into a room; a bold-patterned fabric hung at a window or used to upholster a small piece of furniture will balance a larger piece of plain furniture at the other side of the room.
- Change the apparent size and proportion of a piece of furniture or of an entire room; a sofa covered in a large pattern or bold-colored fabric will appear larger than if it is covered in a dark, plain color or small, all-over pattern. A chair or love seat covered in a vertical stripe will look higher than the same piece covered in plain fabric.
- Change the look of a room for different seasons: a couch and chair in deep warm colors may be slip-covered in light-colored ticking for summer. Heavy winter drapery may be changed for light, sheer glass curtains to create a cool atmosphere for summer.
- Establish the room's color scheme. One of the most successful methods of color-scheming a room is to choose a beautiful patterned fabric as a starting point.
- Establish the authentic style of a room. If your room is based on a certain period, the fabric, more than any other item of furnishing, can set the feeling you wish.
- Add a lot of beauty and comfort in greater measure than any other decorative element.

Fabrics for Period and Contemporary Rooms

The study of textiles is a fascinating one that should occupy no small amount of the homemaker's time and concern. No element can so surely set the general mood of a room as the fabrics, and no element of a room is easier or more often changed. Because of the important role fabric plays in the success of a room, a rather thorough understanding of the use of color, texture, and design in textiles is an absolute necessity. The homemaker should become familiar with the dominant chararacteristics of various period and contemporary fabrics and learn which of these may and may not be combined harmoniously.

Seldom does today's decorator wish to recreate an authentic period room. If your decorative scheme is to be based upon a certain period, you should strive to establish the spirit of that period only, rather than to reproduce it in minute detail. The choice of an authentic fabric will set the spirit or theme of a room more surely than any other decorative element. Documentary designs for any period or style are available, and new and exciting contemporary fabrics are reaching the market every month.

Put Fabric to Work for You

Becoming excited about fabric and what it can do for your home is to become a true decorator. Besides using fabric for all the usual things, expand your imagination and let it do unusual and delightful things for you. Flood a room with a beautiful print by putting it on walls, at the windows, and on several pieces of furniture—you will love it.

Let an appealing multicolor print set your color scheme. Select the lightest, most neutral color for the walls, a deeper color for the carpet. Pull out the other colors for chairs, varying the colors in a small print, a stripe and a plain color. Use some of the most vibrant

Left*: A cozy, comfortable mood is established through the lavish use of informal fabrics. Although several patterns are used, all are informal and a common denominator of color runs through them all. *Courtesy of Ethan Allen.

colors for throw pillows. This recipe for color scheming is infallible.

Try skirting a table for most any room. Don't drape a real table, just fake one instead by topping a barrel with a piece of plywood. The cover can be changed easily with the seasons.

Watch for discontinued samples of unusual fabric and frame a panel on your wall. It is easy to do and can transform an ordinary room into something very special.

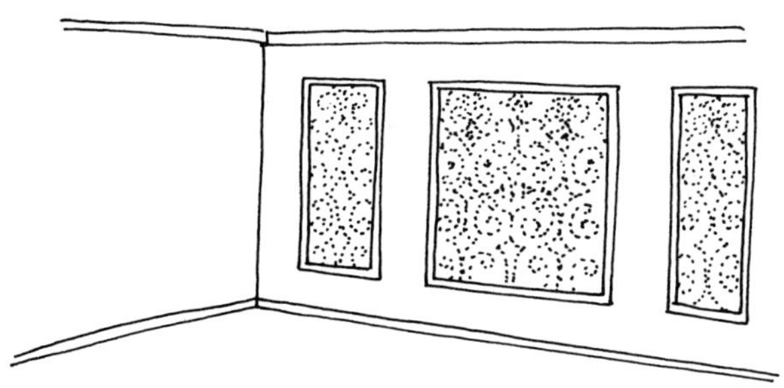

Framed fabrics can change the aspect of a room.

Fabric-covered folding screens can add a touch of beauty and even glamor to your room, and they have a myriad of uses. They can mask an unattractive corner and provide a backdrop for a seating arrangement as well. They can conceal storage, redirect traffic, and serve in lieu of drapery—to mention only a few possibilities.

To give your room a new look for seasons, nothing can accomplish it as surely nor as quickly as slip covers. Select a lively print and cover your sofa and lounge chairs. If you can sew, you can make them yourself; if not, you can have them made. Slip covers can conceal unsightly upholstery or protect delicate fabrics. They can be zipped on and off for cleaning or washing.

Probably the best bargain in fabric today is sheets. No matter what kind of house or apartment you have, consider using them. There is no quicker way to cover large areas so beautifully and economically and with so little effort. Sheets are wide and already hemmed. Use them for walls, bedspreads, dust ruffles, slip covers, drapery, cushions—and even as sheets. Quilt them for comforters, window cornices, or headboards.

The miracles that can be wrought through the skillful and imaginative use of fabric are limitless and await only your enthusiastic efforts.

8
Underfoot--Affordable Beauty and Durability

Laying a new floor is one of the easiest do-it-yourselfers. It requires little or no experience, few tools, and the result can be a custom surface that will retain its new look for years to come, with a minimum of upkeep.

Hard-Surface Flooring

Perhaps the most notable characteristic of today's flooring materials is the merging of beauty and practicality. Time-tested materials such as concrete, terrazzo, quarry, and ceramic tiles have taken on a glamorous quality due to new and improved methods of production, modern developments in the techniques of surface enrichment, and better ways of installation. Larger-sized ceramic tiles are in increasing demand. New setting methods for all types of tile allow installations over most surfaces. Quarry tile and marble, as well as natural stone in aggregate form, continue to supply the demand for beauty, durability, and natural colorations. Hard floor materials are no longer confined to limited areas of the house but may go anywhere. Many are so durable that they may flow from the inside entrance hall or the family room right out onto the porch or patio, thus expanding space, creating unity, and providing a practical surface requiring little upkeep, while at the same time adding beauty to any type of home. There is a new emphasis on wood, and this versatile and timeless flooring is once again in the fashion foreground.

The dramatic development of vinyl for floor use is in large measure responsible for the new interest in hard floor coverings. There is almost no limit to the effects that can and are being produced in vinyl. Vinyl can be clear or can come in literally hundreds of colors, translucent or opaque, textured or satin-smooth. Vinyl comes in tiles, in six-foot-wide sheets, and in cans. It is

Do-it-yourself flooring. ***Below*****: A heavy-duty bricklike floor can be stapled down.** ***Right*****: A vinyl tile floor with self-adhesive for an afternoon's work.** ***Courtesy of Armstrong Cork Co.***

both formal and informal. Until recently, resilient hard-surface floors were used only for kitchens, utility rooms, and bathrooms; today their elegance admits them into any room of the house. Small patterns mask tracking and spillage; pebble vinyls achieve a natural stone effect; and embossed patterns are reminiscent of Old World designs. Vinyls may simulate handsome grained wood, cork, delft tile, travertine, or marble, to mention only a few. There is an all-purpose vinyl in sheet or tile that requires no adhesive. A foam cushion backing makes it possible to have a practical vinyl surface with the luxurious feel of carpet.

The three main choices for hard floor covering are resilient tile, nonresilient tile, and wood.

Resilient Tile

Asbestos Tile. Today's most popular resilient flooring is vinyl asbestos tile. It can be installed anywhere indoors, from basement to attic. Its low cost, availability in a wide variety of colors and patterns, ease of installation, and maintenance account for its continuing popularity. Vinyl asbestos tile has a tight nonporous surface that defies dirt and grease, is durable, and requires little upkeep. For cleaning and installing procedure, follow the manufacturer's directions.

Solid Adhesive-Backed Tiles. Solid vinyl tiles are also in great demand. They come in innumerable styles, and it takes little expertise to simply press them into place. Most vinyl floors have no-wax surfaces; thus, the only maintenance necessary is a damp mop. The cost of solid vinyl is considerably more than asbestos tile, but the effect may be worth it.

Solid Sheet Vinyl. Solid sheet vinyl has the advantage of having few seams, but it requires professional installation.

When selecting a hard-surface material, keep in mind that the surface you install will be a permanent one. Avoid patterns and colors that you may tire of quickly. Select a pattern that lies flat. A three-dimensional design that makes you feel you might trip is uncomfortable to live with.

Non-Resilient Tile

Ceramic Tile. Probably the most exciting development for the home in recent years has been the improvement in ceramic tile. Once used only for bathrooms

Beauty, comfort, and practicality are combined in this cushioned no-wax floor. And it can be installed right over problem floors. *Courtesy of Armstrong Cork Co.*

and counter tops, the new tile styles are creating floors for any area of the house. It comes both glazed and unglazed and in a wide range of sizes, up to twelve-inch squares, that run the full gamut of color.

Quarry Tile. For especially heavy-duty areas, quarry tile is available both glazed and unglazed in four-inch to nine-inch squares, as well as in some curved and geometric shapes.

Kits are available for the person who plans to lay a ceramic- or quarry-tile floor. Your dealer will have for rental all the tools necessary for doing a professional job.

Wood

No other single flooring material has the versatility and timeless appeal of wood. No other floor combines beauty, warmth, resilience, resistance to indentation, durability, availability, and ease of installation. The quiet harmony and beauty of oak floors provide a background for any style of furnishings, and they are always in good taste. Wood has been a favorite choice for centuries, and the decorating trend today favors exposed hardwood with area or room-size rugs.

The conventional method of installing hardwood flooring has been to lay the flooring strips, usually 2½ inches wide and ¾ of an inch thick. This is seldom done today. New developments have virtually eliminated this process. Unit-block flooring is available that comes in both solid hardwood and laminated style. Block flooring has a tongue or a groove on each side (which permits a tight fit). The blocks are available in

Resilient, easy to install, this vinyl simulates the warmth of natural wood. *Courtesy of Perma Grain Products.*

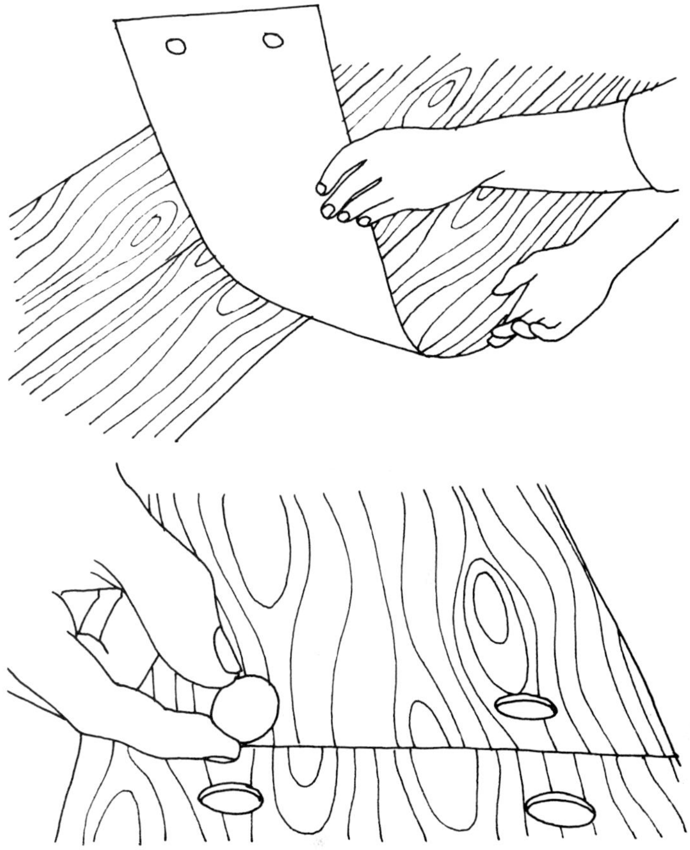

Do-it-yourself, pegs and all.

sizes ranging from 6"×6" to 19"×19". A variety of designs can be achieved, such as basket weave or herringbone. Block flooring comes prefinished and needs only to be dry-mopped. Depending on the amount of use, these floors will need an occasional clean-and-wax job.

Nothing but wood can provide an appropriate flooring for the simplest of rustic furnishings, the most elegant, and everything in between. Once inexpensive, its price in recent years has risen dramatically. But once it is down, wood is forever, and it gets more beautiful with wear and care.

For a perfect floor in which you can take pride, follow the manufacturer's directions. Any equipment you need to do the job can be rented at a reasonable cost.

If you live in a house built before the 1950's, chances are you have a hardwood floor under your wall-to-wall carpeting. Take a look! If you are fortunate enough to find hardwood, you may wish to consider using an area or room-size rug when you recarpet. No matter what the style of your furnishings, or if they are no style at all, a hardwood floor will enhance them.

Restoring a scuffed or dingy floor to its original beauty may be a minor undertaking or it may require involved refinishing, in which case it may be wise to consult a professional. In either case, the result, a beautiful hardwood floor, will be well worth the effort and the expense.

Soft Flooring

So you have decided to buy a new carpet? Wait a minute! How much thought have you given to this important purchase? What do you know about carpet fibers? Do you know which ones wear the best, are the most resilient, shed dirt, clean well, and fit your budget? Have you considered color or pattern? Where are you going to shop? If the answers to any of these ques-

Right: For elegant dining, French Provincial furniture on a Kirman rug create a room both formal and livable. The rich wood paneling provides an appropriate foil for the soft colors of the drapery, chair covering, furniture, and rug. *Courtesy of Thomasville Furniture, Inc.*

tions are not clear to you, do a little investigating. Read on!

Since the 1960s, there has been an unprecedented boom in the carpet industry. This is partially accounted for by the improved fibers with properties that people have demanded and at prices they can afford. Of all the household furnishings, carpeting may be the one of greatest concern. Certainly it is one of the largest investments the homeowner makes, and with the wide variety of available fibers and floor fashions, the consumer often becomes confused.

Considerations When Selecting Carpet

The things to be considered when you are planning to buy carpet for your home are: quality and cost, where to buy, where it will be used, the color and pattern, and the required size or amount.

Quality

How long do you plan to live in your present home? Granted, permanency is never absolutely sure, but if you expect to move within a year or two it is a mistake to put a lot of money into a carpet. It will make little or no difference to the resale value of your home, so find an inexpensive but attractive one to serve temporarily. On the other hand, if you feel that you are reasonably permanent, the best quality carpet you can afford will be your best investment.

How does one judge quality? Quality today is dependent upon four basic ingredients: (1) Type and grade of fiber, (2) The depth of the pile, (3) The density of the pile, and (4) Construction.

Fibers. Four fibers account for most carpets made today:

- Wool is the luxury fiber and where price is no consideration, wool is the most desirable carpet fiber. It is durable, soil resistant, resilient, and warm; it cleans well; and it takes color beautifully. But, because of the high price, wool is restricted to the few who can afford it.
- Nylon is the biggest seller of all the fibers. It wears better than any other fiber, is soil resistant, and cleans well. It has been the least expensive fiber, but it is moving up in price as manufacturing methods have improved.
- Acrylic is durable, cleans well, and for a time was next to nylon in quantity sold, but has fallen off in recent years.
- Polyester is presently on the increase in volume. It costs slightly less than nylon, is durable, soil resistant, and cleans well, but has a visible sheen. When polyester and nylon are blended in equal amounts, they produce an excellent carpet that is more like wool than any other combination of fibers, and the sheen that is characteristic of 100 percent polyester is obscured.
- Olefin has been especially popular for kitchens and indoor-outdoor carpets, but recently is being replaced by nylon.

Carpet prices vary in different areas of the country and with the national inflation. To quote any specific costs would be folly.

Depth of Pile. Because deeper pile requires more yarn, the deeper the pile, the more durable the carpet.

Density of Pile. The more dense the surface, the better the carpet will wear. Examine the density—the number of threads per square inch—by bending back a piece of carpet. If there are wide spaces between the threads or wide gaps between rows and large amounts of backing showing, the carpet, in all probability, will not wear well.

Construction. Because of the many new technical developments, the old and well-known weaves no longer account for the bulk of present-day carpets. Most carpets on the market today are tufted. The Axminster, a woven carpet that for a number of years was used very little, is again a popular patterned floor covering. It wears well. A combination of 80 percent wool and 20 percent nylon is especially desirable in the new Axminster carpets.

Where to Buy

Go to a reputable dealer in whom you have confidence. Reputable dealers will assure you of the quality you are buying, will handle and guarantee a satisfactory installation, and will stand behind their products.

Look for the label bearing the generic name that assures you of the fiber content. Buy a dependable brand. Look for a label on the carpet that gives the name of an established manufacturer. This is your assurance of obtaining good value in the price range you select. Some manufacturers offer warrantees of five to ten years on their carpets. Make inquiry about this, and be sure to save the warranty card.

Avoid package deals with costs of carpet, installation, and padding lumped together. Find out the price

per square yard as well as the charges for installation and padding. Never rely on door-to-door or telephone salesmen.

Where It Will be Used

Before deciding on the surface characteristic of the carpet, consider the area to be carpeted, the size of the room, by whom it will be used, for what purposes, and the amount of traffic. If the area is small, wall-to-wall carpeting in a solid color or an all-over texture will give the room a feeling of spaciousness. For a larger room, a pattern is appropriate but it will restrict your choice of drapery and upholstery. In a living room where traffic is limited and a more serene and formal atmosphere is desired, a plain "splush"—a pile between shag and plush—may be your preference. For heavy traffic areas such as family rooms, stairways, and rooms used as passageways, choose good quality carpet that wears well, is crush-resistant, and resists soil. Tweeds in tight loop pile are an excellent choice here. Shag carpet that flooded the market for a number of years is all but gone. An embossed pattern—woven high and low—is coming on strong. It is practical, hides footprints, and masks spots. Berber carpets are particularly popular for modern interiors. Their earthy tones create suitable backgrounds for a wide range of colors.

Color and Pattern

Color in a carpet is of vital importance, because the floor is the largest usable area of the room, is the least often changed, and is the background for all other furnishings. The light has an effect upon the color; therefore, it must be considered. A sunny room may call for a carpet in a cool color or a deep shade. For a northern exposure or a dark room, one of the warm colors in a lighter tone may be a better choice. Before you make a final decision, take home samples of the carpets you like best. Keep them overnight to observe the colors and textures in your own environment. See them in the daylight, both morning and afternoon, and under artificial light. The change that occurs from the store to your home will amaze you.

Keep in mind that plain and darker colors will show dust and spots more than lighter neutral tones. Soft earthy tones are in greater supply today than they have been in years. Avocado and brassy gold, that were so fashionable for a number of years, have lost favor—which is the way with fashion. Always beware of

A handcrafted quilt look is created with this do-it-yourself American patchwork carpet. Its nylon pile offers excellent wear, hides soil, and is at home wherever lively color and informality are desired. *Courtesy of Armstrong Cork Co.*

faddish "in" colors that you see demonstrated everywhere. You can be sure the "Joneses" will use them and their houses will all look alike. Choose colors that you and your family enjoy and that are right for your particular needs. If you choose nice "dirty" colors, they will be easy to live with and will never go out of style. They will mask soil so that upkeep will be minimal. They will provide a good background for a wide variety of colors, fabrics, and accessories. And if you want a new mood, you can achieve it without having to change your floor covering.

All kinds of patterned carpets are on the market today, and they are gaining in popularity. Designs are available that are appropriate for any type or style of room. A new printing process that is basically a screen-printing technique has contributed to the interest in patterned floors.

While examining the rolls or carpet samples, look for a little tag that says, "Soil resistant, protected with Scotchgard." This does not mean that your carpet will not get soiled, but the surface treatment will help to keep it clean for a long time.

Carpet squares are a practical solution to a high-cost carpet installation. The result can be a customized luxurious floor, easily done by the average do-it-yourselfer. *Courtesy of Armstrong Cork Co.*

Your carpets are usually the biggest investment you will make in your home. You will live with them for a long time, so choose them wisely. Then enjoy them—and don't wear them out cleaning them.

Rug Size

Wall-to-Wall. When carpeting is installed wall-to-wall, there are some distinct advantages; it creates continuity within a room or from room to room, makes rooms look larger, adds warmth and a feeling of luxury, requires only one cleaning process, and provides maximum safety from accidents. But there are also some accompanying disadvantages; it must be cleaned on the floor; it cannot be turned for even wear; and only part can be salvaged if moved.

In recent years, the cost of carpet installation has been on the increase—until at present the cost of installation sometimes equals the carpet itself—and sometimes actually exceeds it. Carpet layers are often in short supply because they are generally members of a high-paid union that is tightly controlled.

Room Size. A room-size rug comes within a few inches of the walls, leaving a marginal strip of floor exposed. There are standard size rugs to fit most rooms. Nine by twelve rugs are probably the most common, but you can, without any problem, have a rug made any size you need. The room-size rug has most of the advantages that wall-to-wall carpeting has, plus some extra benefits, not the least of which is the fact that there is no installation fee, since you can lay it yourself. Another advantage is that it can be turned for even distribution of wear, removed for cleaning, and you can take it with you if you move. The floor, however, does require two cleaning processes—one for the rug and one for the exposed wood. If the floor is not hardwood, it can be successfully camouflaged with one of the hard surface materials that simulate wood, such as tile, brick, or whatever surface is the most appropriate for your room.

Area Rug. An area rug is one that does not cover the entire floor but is used to define an area of a room according to its function. The rug should be large enough to accommodate all the furniture used in the area grouping.

Carpet Squares. Carpet squares are now available as a solution to the high cost of carpet installation. Carpet squares can be laid down permanently, semi-permanently, or merely pressed into position and picked up for cleaning or replacement if a serious mishap occurs. The most popular carpet tile is one made of olefin fiber, backed with adhesive with a protective covering. These floor coverings are especially practical for family and recreation rooms and children's rooms.

Art Rug. An art rug is generally handcrafted and used as an accent, or treated as a focal point. Often it is placed so furniture does not encroach upon it, enabling it to be admired like a picture on the floor. With the current interest in, and revival of, all manner of handicrafts, you may at this time have a hooked rug partly done on a loom.

Carpet Underlay

A good carpet underlay gives tremendous value for the money spent, and every carpet deserves one. Furthermore, cushioning improves and helps to maintain the appearance of the carpet, enhances the resiliency that assists in preventing matting of the pile, and prolongs the life of the carpet by as much as 75 percent. It absorbs noise and creates a feeling of luxury. Even low or moderately priced carpet, when laid over a good pad, will take on a feeling of cushioned elegance.

There are a number of basic types of underlay on the market. Your dealer will recommend the best one for your particular purpose.

Oriental Rugs

The making of Oriental rugs is one of the great arts of the world, and these rugs are appreciated by discriminating people everywhere. Oriental rugs have been coveted possessions for hundreds of years, and proud owners have found that the joy of living with them increases with the years. With the advent of wall-to-wall carpeting, however, Oriental rugs went out of fashion in America. But now, after having languished in warehouse and attics for a number of decades, they have been rediscovered and once again taken their place as high-fashion floor coverings. Oriental rugs are the most versatile of floor coverings, and they will outwear any commercially made carpet. Many discriminating people are finding these handsome carpets highly desirable for contemporary homes. During the first half of this century, Oriental rugs could be purchased at private auction for unbelievably low prices but today the cost has skyrocketed. The great majority of Oriental rugs imported into America in the past came from Iran (Persia) and Turkey. But in recent years, many are coming from India where the low labor cost makes it possible to produce wool rugs in Persian and Turkish designs for much less than those made in the near east.

If you are considering an Oriental rug, by all means do some careful studying before making a purchase. You may then be fortunate enough to make a good buy at a local auction. When once you have lived with a beautiful Oriental rug, you will never want to be without one. Their beauty, remarkable wearing quality, and versatility make them heirlooms to be passed from one generation to another.

To meet the current demand, American manufacturers are duplicating authentic Oriental design in loom-woven rugs that retail at prices within the budget of the average purchaser. These are usually made of wool and called "American Orientals." They can be very handsome and will give you much aesthetic pleasure.

Carpet Care

To get the most enjoyment and wear from your carpet, you should give it proper care and cleaning. The amount of use will determine the frequency of vacuuming, but remember that it is the sand and dirt particles that become lodged in the pile that cut the fibers. Remove spots immediately—be sure to find out from your dealer when you make your purchase what cleaner to use. Different fibers require different cleaners. Don't have your new carpet cleaned until it is absolutely necessary! It will never be quite the same after a cleaning and too much cleaning can be damaging. As with all of your household cleaning, use your common sense in taking care of your carpets.

9
Ways with Walls

When you walk into a room, you meet the walls at eye level and you cannot avoid seeing them. The walls of a room occupy the largest area. They serve the function of protection and privacy, and they are the background for fabrics and furniture; but most important, they provide the background for people.

Rooms in which people spend little time, such as foyers, may have success with backgrounds in bold and dramatic patterns. Rooms for relaxing are better if the backgrounds are unobtrusive. Some walls emphasize openness and informality. Others stress protection and formality. Aesthetically, walls contribute significantly to the success of a room and to the general atmosphere and personality.

Today's Rigid Wall Coverings

The materials available for wall treatments today are more varied and plentiful than ever before. Each type has advantages and disadvantages with regard to appearance, cost, upkeep, noise insulation, and longevity. The important thing in making a choice is that the wall materials are appropriate for the particular room since the wall treatment determines in large measure the general scheme of the room.

Some wall treatments are extremely versatile, while others belong to certain moods and period styles. Heavy masonry is most appropriately used in large contemporary rooms and calls for large-scale furniture, heavily textured fabrics, and strong colors. There is a current vogue for natural textures, and brick and stone are used abundantly both inside and out. Brick has been used since the time of the pharaohs and has a timeless quality of warmth and adaptability to many styles.

Stone is less warm than brick, but its durability and strength make it particularly desirable for contemporary rooms. (It is also at home in many rooms with a traditional but rustic atmosphere.) Plaster has been used for centuries, but today the expense makes it prohibitive in low-cost housing. Sheetrock is now commonly used instead, but when it has been painted, it produces the effect of plaster. Different finishing techniques can produce a variety of effects from very rough to very smooth. Because the plain wall can be used almost anywhere, it is the safest background to use in rooms where furnishings may likely be changed from time to time.

The plain-walled shoebox look, which held sway from about the 1920s to the 1950s is no longer the fashion. The decorative background has been reestablished. Paint, paper, and wood paneling—the time-tested standbys—have been much improved and are in great demand, but the market also abounds with new materials. For example, new techniques in preparing and installing all types of masonry have increased its usefulness. A renaissance in ceramic tiles has produced patterns, textures, and shapes for every room and purpose. New metal tiles of steel, copper, and aluminum are available for many areas.

There is a new emphasis on wood paneling. Solid wood planking is costly and requires custom labor, but there are many satisfactory substitutes. Veneered panels that are beautifully grained, factory finished, and available at reasonable prices are ready for easy installation. Hardboard and plastic laminate panels, simulating real wood but impervious to dents, are available at unbelievably low cost.

To satisfy the current demand for architectural interest, manufacturers have made available many items to be applied to walls. Stock moldings are available which, when applied, give the impression of a dado or complete period paneling. There is a three-dimensional composition material so lightweight it can be glued into place. It is made to resemble carved cornices, moldings, and boiseries, or it may cover a wide area to simulate brick or stone. This decoration stands out in sharp relief and is amazingly realistic. When skillfully used, it adds interest, dimension, and period effects to otherwise plain walls. Lightweight beams of polyurethane provide an authentic look of Rural English or French Manor or just a rustic atmosphere. When glued against plastic ceilings, they appear uncannily like old hand-hewn wood.

Just-for-fun wallpaper should delight both young and old. The vinyl coating makes finger marks and spots no problem. *Courtesy of Imperial Wallcoverings.*

Wallpaper

Nothing can so quickly and surely change the appearance of a room as giving it a covering of wallpaper, and the choice has never been so great as at the present time. Today's wall coverings are virtually exploding with variety, beauty, and practicality. Patterns, styles, and surface effects are unlimited. There are photo murals for one wall or more restrained murals designed to be used continuously on four walls, thus deepening the prespective of a room. There are three-dimensional wall coverings that look like straw matting, bamboo, wood, brick, stone, marble, tortoise shell, and so on. There are papers to add architectural dimension to your rooms, as well as everything from authentic period designs to super graphics. And, in spite of their beauty and elegance, these new wallpapers have a practicality never dreamed of a few years ago.

For today's practical decorator, there are numerous flexible wallpapers treated with varying thickness of vinyl and made to simulate any type of wall covering, rig-

Below: What could make a sewing corner more pleasant than to cover the wall, window lambrequin, and chair with a delicate floral print? Another example of attic space put to good use. *Courtesy of The Warner Co. Right*: Wallpaper makes the room. Here a striking geometric is used on the wall, on the folding divider, and on the cupboard doors. The white wood trim and floor-length table cover pick up the colors from the paper. *Courtesy of The Warner Co.*

id or nonrigid. They may be washable or scrubbable; they are waterproof, highly durable, and stain resistant; and they can be used on nearly any type of wall. These vinyl papers or fabric-backed coverings are applied the same as wallpaper, but unlike paper they can be stripped off walls and even reused.

Wallpaper Terms

Because wallpaper plays such an important role in today's decorating, and because many a person at one time or another will purchase and even try hanging paper, it is wise to be familiar with some common terms.

- Washable. Usually refers to a wall covering that may be washed with lukewarm, mild suds, but not scrubbed excessively.
- Scrubbable. Refers to wall covering more resistant to rubbing than the washable types. Stains such as crayon marks can generally be removed from scrubbable materials with cleaning agents recommended by the manufacturer or with soap and water.
- Pretrimmed. Refers to rolls of wallpaper from which the selvage has been trimmed.
- Semitrimmed. Means that the selvage has been trimmed from one edge only.
- Prepasted. Paper has had paste applied during the manufacturing process. Detailed instructions for hanging are usually included.
- Single roll. Wallpaper is always priced by the single roll but is usually sold by the double or triple roll. Regardless of width, a single roll contains thirty-six square feet. Why this curious pricing persists no one seems to know.
- Strippable. This means it can be peeled off without injuring the wall.
- Double and triple rolls. Regardless of width, a double roll contains 72 square feet, and a triple roll contains 108 square feet. Some expensive papers may be purchased by the yard.

Yes—*you* can do your own wallpapering. It may put a strain on your patience, but the feeling of accomplishment you will experience will be well worth the effort.

When you select your paper, be sure to check the "printing run" number in case you need to order more. The color varies slightly with each "run." It is wise to over order and return the full rolls you do not use.

Be sure to use the right kind of paste. The old standby, wheat paste, works best on most paper; but vinyl wall coverings require a vinyl adhesive. Check with your dealer about this and about the amount of paper you will need.

Fabrics for Walls

Fabric for walls is by no means a new idea. It has been used on walls for centuries to provide warmth and elegance, and it has simply returned to fashion. Many fabrics with paper backing come prepared for easy application. Commonplace materials such as burlap, ticking, felt, and many others can add charm to the traditional and modern rooms. Damasks and other fabrics with documentary designs can set the feeling of authenticity to period rooms. Fabric not only adds character and beauty but insulates against sound. Your best choice, except when using the shirred method of application, is a medium-weight, closely woven fabric such as sailcloth, burlap, ticking, felt, Indian head, or glazed chintz. Allover, nondirectional patterns are the easiest to use, since they require no matching. Where a repeat pattern is used, it will be necessary (as with wallpaper) to allow for matching.

Ways of Applying Fabric to Walls

There are several methods of applying fabric to walls, any one of which you can do yourself. Try one of the following methods:

Shirring Method. This is the simplest way to cover a wall with fabric. The result is a pretty effect and one that is easy to take down and clean. First, fasten cut-to-fit rods just above the baseboard and near the ceiling. Cut single lengths of fabric, allowing three inches top and bottom for headings. Gather the material the same as for sash curtains.

Masking-Tape Method. This method is not a permanent one since masking tape will dry out in time. Prepare fabric by sewing together and pressing seams. Stick tape around edges of the wall, peel off the outer coat, then apply the fabric first top and bottom and then the sides. Take care to keep the straight grain of the material vertical.

Velcro Method. This is similar to the masking-tape method except that one side of the velcro tape is stitched along the edges of the fabric then attached to the other side of the tape which has been placed around the edges of the wall.

Staple Method. Prepare fabric as in masking-tape method. Staple top first, then bottom, and lastly the sides. Exposed staples may be concealed with braid or molding.

Paste Method. This is the most professional looking and most permanent method but also requires special care. For this method you will need a set of wallpaper tools. The wall should be prepared by a coat of modocol. When you are ready to apply the lengths of fabric, paint a second coat of modocol on the first section, place the first strip of fabric as you would with wallpaper, and proceed in this manner. When the job is completed, allow to dry overnight then spray with one of the protective materials.

Whichever method you use for application, if the fabric is carefully chosen, your room will be enhanced.

Other Flexible Wall Coverings

In addition to wallpaper and fabric, a number of other flexible wall coverings are on the market.

Japanese Grass

Japanese grass cloth is a beautiful, long-lasting, and easy-to-care-for wall covering that provides a background for a variety of decorating schemes. However, it would not be a good choice in areas where little hands would likely rub over it; nor does the cloth hold color well.

Leather

Real leather is available for walls, but the cost is often prohibitive.

Cork

Cork is a handsome, textured, moderately high-priced material. It produces a warm atmosphere in natural colors of brown. It is particularly adaptable for studies and rooms where sound insulation is important.

Carpet

Carpet is now going up the walls and even onto the ceilings. Carpet material made especially for walls is slightly thinner than typical carpeting and comes in both squares and yardage. Adhesives and proper installation methods are still being developed; but considering the aesthetic and acoustical values that wall

Weathered barn-wood walls and an open-beamed ceiling set the mood for this added-on family room. Quarry tile floor, rough textured upholstery and large-scale, easily movable furniture create a room that is fun for the whole family. *Courtesy of Drexel Heritage Furnishings.*

carpeting offers, it promises to become one of the important new developments of the last quarter of the twentieth-century. Hemp-woven carpet for walls adds texture or pattern. It spot cleans and muffles sound.

Change the Visual Aspect of a Room with Paper or Fabric on the Wall

Through no other means can the visual aspect of a room be so completely established as through the use of a wallpaper or fabric and the things they can accomplish are many. They can

- Bring beauty and charm into an otherwise dreary room.
- Add interesting architectural details by the use of a wallpaper which simulates such architectural details as pilasters, cornices, dadoes, and latticework.
- Establish a specific period through the use of an authentic motif.
- Set the mood of a room. Through the use of refined pattern, neutralized colors, and smooth texture, the mood becomes formal. Through the use of quaint, realistic patterns and lively colors, the mood becomes informal.

Japanese grass cloth is a perfect background for the bold contemporary print on the love seat. Shuttered windows, hardwood floor, and geometric patterned area rug all contribute to the natural look in which the accessories feel "at home." *Courtesy of Kaylyn, Inc.*

- Make a room appear masculine, with horizontal lines, bold patterns, and strong colors; or feminine, with curved lines, delicate patterns, and pastel colors.
- Supply a dramatic focus to a room needing some excitement by the use of striking murals or a framed panel of exceptional paper or fabric.
- Conceal architectural defects by the use of a small allover pattern.
- Bring harmony into a room by the use of a paper that will unify the different components of the room.
- Add interest and sparkle to a room by the use of "just for fun" paper.
- Change the apparent size and proportion of a room, that is, make it appear larger, smaller, higher, or lower.

Before deciding on a paper or a fabric for your walls, study your room carefully. Try to visualize the room as it will look. It will be helpful to examine pictures of rooms, similar to your own, with papered walls. It can prepare you for the great change that will take place in the atmosphere of the room. If you have made a careful choice of paper or fabric, the result should be one to give you years of pleasure.

Despite the area they occupy, your walls can be changed with less effort and for less expense than your furniture, floor covering, or any other decorative element in your home. And the wonders you can bring about through well-chosen wall treatments present a real challenge.

10 Where There's a Window, There's a Way

Are windows a problem for you? Cheer up! Things have changed. True, there was a time not so long ago when problem windows *were* just that. But not any more—thanks to the new freedom in window decorating. Today, if your windows are too big or too little, too high or too low, too many or too few, or if they are badly proportioned or placed in such a way that they throw the room out of balance, you need not be unduly concerned. Often a window that is an architectural liability can be turned into an asset. Simply visualize the room's elevations as you would *like* them to look, then proceed to make them *look* that way. If a wall has no window, it can be treated as if it had.

Changing a window treatment can give your room a completely new dimension, and it needn't strain the budget excessively. A nondescript room can take on glamour and beauty with a dramatic splash of fabric at the window. A busy room can become quiet, and a small room will expand when windows are inconspicuously draped or shuttered to blend into a neutral background.

No shape or size of window should cause undue concern. It is no trick to make small windows appear larger: simply hang drapery floor to ceiling to add height, and carry drapery out on the wall to create the appearance of width.

The Large Window

A very large window sometimes requires special attention. In some climates, it can admit too much heat in summer and too much cold in winter. Glare from a large expanse of glass can cause discomfort, excessive light bleaches furnishings, and a blank wall of glass at nighttime is unattractive.

The most common treatment here is to use a casement, plain or loosely woven, that admits some light

Ceiling-high windows add dignity to the neoclassical room. Unobtrusive draperies appropriately reveal the small panes. The pedestal tables, Louis XVI arm chair, and urn lamp establish the mood commonly called Italian Provincial. *Courtesy of Henredon Furniture Industries, Inc.*

Windows without drapery or shutters. When a window looks onto a view and there is no need for privacy, to do nothing but use plants and furniture is sometimes the best thing. The graceful deer placed on the table adds special interest. *Courtesy of J. P. Hogan & Co.*

when drawn during the daytime and provides privacy at night. The objection to this treatment is that when drapery is drawn during the daytime, the view is obstructed.

One answer to that objective is to use sheers. Once common to most homes, the sheer, or glass curtain, is again in favor. Sheers hang permanently against the glass and will cut glare, filter the light, add softness to the room—but still permit a view. They are appropriate for both modern and traditional rooms. However, some provision, such as an under-draw will be necessary here to give nighttime privacy (unless side-draw draperies are used).

The fiber most widely used for sheers is polyester. It is tub-washable and dripdry, requires no ironing, and holds up under direct sunlight. Ninon, voile, and batiste are three favorite polyester sheers. Many fabrics are being produced in wider widths today to take care of oversized windows.

Another solution to the big window is louvered blinds or shutters in either vertical or horizontal style. These can be used alone or with side drapery.

The Bay Window

An important element in many traditional homes, the bay window is being used again with success in many styles of architecture. It permits light from three directions, makes a room seem physically larger, and adds a dramatic touch. There are no particular rules about the treatment of bay windows. Use your own good ideas. The simple design is usually the best. Beware of swags here (or anywhere for that matter). In some formal rooms, swags may be appropriate, but frequently when they are used to give the supposed impression of elegance, the result is disastrous.

Informal to formal—three solutions for awkward windows.

That Odd Little Window

What about those little off-beat windows tucked into awkward places, but where the light they emit is necessary? Why not have some fun with one. Cover the entire wall with fabric or shutters or make a feature of its littleness. Paint a super graphic around it and leave the window bare. Let your imagination run riot in the choice of a graphic.

Exposed hard-edged lines framing deep-set windows need no drapery here. Roll-up woven window shades control the light for a plant-filled room. *Courtesy of Clopay Corp.*

The Many Uses of Shutters

One of the most versatile of all window treatments, the louvered shutter has never been in more demand than at present. To fill the great demand, many variations are being produced. Use them to cover any size window, or an entire wall to give the illusion of a window where there is none.

Try flanking a window with shutters, or use make-it-yourself movable screens that can be as tailored or as dramatic as you choose. The bonus with standing shutters and screens is that they go with you and can be used at other windows or for a myriad of other purposes. Screens are one of the great decorating tools.

What is more versatile than shutters? They go in any style of room and on any kind of window. In addition to adding beauty, they can adjust to expose the view, give complete privacy, or to allow any amount of light. ***Courtesy of Henredon Furniture Industries, Inc.***

One style of shutter currently very popular is made of very slender slats that can afford any degree of light control or complete privacy if desired. When the tiny slats are open, the shutter seems to completely disappear, permitting a view. These shutters or blinds are durable, come in almost any color, and can be used with or without drapery. They are at home in any room, at any window, or where there is no window at all. You can even use them for room dividers or to conceal storage. They can provide a definite design statement in your room.

Other Window Solutions

Once used almost entirely for functional purposes, the window shade today is serving double duty. Decorative window shades are available in an array of fresh or muted colors, bold modern and documentary designs, and with unusual fabrics and trims. Some are laminated fabrics with vinyl coating; others are vinyl impregnated and scrubbable. Many are coordinated with drapery and wall fabrics. Used alone or in combinations with drapery or sheers, they can add color, interest, and glamor while serving a useful purpose—and they are easy to make!

The Roman shade is essentially a more decorative version of a roller shade and can be both stylish and practical. Cafe curtains are one answer when you need both light and privacy at the same time. Usually considered informal, they can lend almost any decorative note you wish. They can be plain, ruffled, tucked,

Take one little window.

trimmed with plain or print bands. They can be two-tiered, three-tiered, with or without valances. They can be hung on rods, with big rings or with clip-on rings or with decorative bands to form loops.

Where heat and cold are no problem, try getting the maximum benefit from nature's decorating. Try undressing your windows and hanging plants at varying heights to create a bower of greenery. When the sunlight streams through, the effect will lift your spirits.

Let Drapery Cut Your Utility Bills

With the energy consciousness of the American public and people everywhere looking for ways to insulate their windows from the seasonal elements, curtains and draperies can play an important role. Curtain and drapery manufacturers have produced a variety of insulators for windows to save energy, such as double woven, multilayered effects that trap warm air in the room and insulated linings and insulated drapery that reduce the amount of heat and cold, thus cutting down on utility bills.

Close the louvered drapery and you have a mural. Open it and you have a full view. Or you can adjust it to admit any amount of light you wish, from either the right or the left. ***Courtesy of Louver Drape.***

Drapery—A Number One Do-It-Yourself Project

One of the most successful ways to save money when transforming a room is by making and installing your own draperies. The first step is to study your window carefully to determine the style of drapery and the type of fabric that best meets your needs. Then, become familiar with drapery hardware. It is available for any style or size of window and for any type of treatment. Check with your hardware or drapery department for suggestions and brochures.

It is a wise procedure to select and mount the hardware before taking the final measurements for your drapery. Don't skimp on yardage. Much of the beauty of drapery lies in its abundant folds. It is better to use a less expensive fabric with ample fulness than a more costly fabric with insufficient fulness. Keep in mind that the key to successful decorating is fabric and nowhere is it more evident than at the window. How-to booklets on making and hanging drapery are available at little cost.

What could be more delightful than a Raggedy Ann shade, topped by a plain valance, in a Raggedy Ann room for a young child? *Courtesy of Clopay Corp.*

There are fabrics to solve any window problem. New magic fabrics that are dripdry, sun resistant, and soil repellant have eliminated the old concern for upkeep. Ready-made curtains and draperies are easily obtainable at modern cost. Remember that there are no absolute musts about window decoration. But do keep in mind that windows face two ways: in *and* out. Many people see your windows from the outside; only a comparatively few see them on the inside. Patterned fabric must always be lined if the windows look onto the street. A plain, off-white lining will make windows unobtrusive. Where several windows face the street, they ought to look as much alike as possible, especially those on the same exposure and on the same level.

Do not be afraid to use your imagination. Put your own individuality into your windows. In no other place will it pay off so much. Dare to be daring. It will give you a lift. And always keep in mind that, "Where there's a window, there's a way to decorate it."

11
Furniture-- Faddish or Forever

Furnishing one's home can be one of life's real pleasures, and each step should be enjoyed and taken with the future in mind. Each furniture purchase should be made only after careful study and planning. Some furniture looks beautiful and is relatively inexpensive but is not well made, while some less expensive furniture that may not have the same surface appearance is well constructed. To become a discriminating customer takes time and effort, but it will pay big dividends. If you are knowledgeable about what constitutes good design and what goes into the making of a fine piece of furniture, you will make a wiser choice, and what you choose may well be a joy forever.

To choose the good from the faddish should be the aim of every homemaker. Look for simple but well-designed pieces. Avoid buying a room full of advertised "economy" furniture. At best, it will be mediocre and likely will be dated in a few years. Remember that decorating is a continuing process: your circumstances change, you will need more furniture. Choose one piece at a time, and select each piece with your general theme in mind. Resist the temptation to get something that is momentarily appealing but in no way related to your other furnishings. Don't be carried away by an overwhelming sales pitch or a so-called bargain. Remember that, no matter what the cost, if a piece of furniture does not fill your needs and does not "feel" right in your room, it is not a bargain. Always shop with a tape measure. Know the space you have to fill and choose furniture with the correct scale in mind.

Furniture Marketing Methods

Some understanding of furniture marketing methods will be helpful in making a purchase. For example, most furniture is presented to the customer in suites, groups, and collections.

A *suite* consists of pieces of furniture designed to be used together in a specific room. All pieces look alike and are priced as a unit, and as a rule they cannot be broken up. Two such units are a dining room suite, consisting of a table, chairs, and a buffet, and a bedroom suite, consisting of a bed, chest, and a dresser.

A *furniture group* is a large ensemble or collection correlated by the same design. A group may include suites for bedrooms, dining rooms, and living rooms, and it might include many extra pieces. The advantage in purchasing from a group is that pieces are coordinated, and additional items are available at any time to complete your starter set. There is danger here, however, that the look-alike feeling will become monotonous or even overpowering if the furniture is heavy. Avoid rooms in which everything matches; they lack interest and personality. You can find plenty of such rooms set up in furniture stores.

A *collection* has the look of individuality and is usually in the higher-priced market. The impression here is one of a mixture of pieces thoughtfully collected over a period of time. Designs are not the same, but all will have a feeling of compatibility.

Because there are so many hidden values in furniture construction, it is important that you buy from a reputable dealer and, whenever possible, choose brand names that you have seen advertised nationally. Most manufacturers now supply information tags and literature with their furniture. Read all such tags carefully and check the guarantees.

Buying Wood Furniture

The price of a piece of furniture is related to the actual value, with reference to the *wood used, quality of construction, finish,* and *design.* Beyond these, you are paying for various refinements such as hand carving, unusual veneers, exotic woods, and luxury fabrics.

Know the Wood

In order to determine the type of wood used in a piece of furniture, become familiar with those kinds most commonly used. Also, learning the wood terms *solid, genuine,* and *veneer* will help you buy wisely. A piece of furniture marked "solid" is made from solid hardwood. The label "genuine" shows that the furniture is made of a single hardwood, with veneer on flat surfaces and solid structural parts, such as the legs. Veneer is a thin layer of finishing wood applied to the body of a less refined wood. Some people still cling to the old notion that furniture with veneer is of inferior quality. Quite the contrary is true. With the new methods of cutting and laminating veneers, a piece of veneered furniture today can be stronger and more resistant to warping than a solid piece. Only veneering permits the beautiful effects achieved by the different methods of matching wood grains.

Hardwoods such as maple, walnut, mahogany, and teak are more durable and dent resistant than soft woods such as pine. They are also more beautiful and more costly but are well worth the difference.

Construction Quality

The quality of construction, which ranges from poor to excellent, often must be left to the integrity of the manufacturer and the word of the salesperson. A reliable merchant will be honest in his evaluation of the furniture he sells. The success of his business depends upon it. (Read "Buying Case Goods" through "Buying Upholstered Furniture," pp. 82–84.)

Finish

The finish on a piece of wood furniture is not always evident, but with a little study one can become a fairly good judge on the basis of appearance. Good furniture has a mellow patina that is produced only by much rubbing, a practice that requires time and effort and therefore adds to the total cost. There are a number of finishes used on furniture today to help maintain the beauty of the wood and protect it against the hazards of daily use. They make woods highly resistant to marks from glasses, spills, scratches, and abraisions. Even cigarette burns no longer hold the dread for a hostess that they once did. These wonder-working finishes are often completely invisible and let the beauty of the wood grain and the color shine through. Ask the salesperson about the surface finish; he or she should be qualified to explain the type of finish on the furniture you are considering. Poorly constructed furniture often has a hard shine produced by varnish that may cover inferior wood but will quickly show scratches.

Design

Design is a personal thing, but furniture should be chosen on the basis of good design, individual preference, and suitability. Look for simple, unadorned furniture. It will very likely be a better value than ornate pieces. Avoid purchasing cheap imitations of more costly hand-carved items.

Sturdy, livable, and in good taste, this comfortable sitting area has appeal for all ages. Simple lined furniture and long-wearing, easily cleaned fabrics relieve the strain from heavy use. *Courtesy of Hercules, Inc.*

Know what is good design, what you like, and what is right for your needs. If a piece of furniture does not appeal to you, no matter how "in" it may be, do not be pressured into buying it. *Remember that you do not have to pay a lot for good design.* It is quite possible to get furniture that is desirable and well designed for a modest price if you are willing to forego unnecessary extras and take time to do some comparison shopping. Put your money into quality. Buy good furniture once, and it will grow more beautiful with use and care. Buy cheap furniture, and you will have to buy again and again and may never enjoy complete satisfaction.

Buying Case Goods

You can make an expert decision when buying case goods if you are well aware of what constitutes quality of construction. Look for the following:

- Examine the drawers. A quality piece will have well-fitted, dovetail joints, sides of the drawers will be smoothly sanded and waxed, and there will be blocks glued underneath the corners to prevent

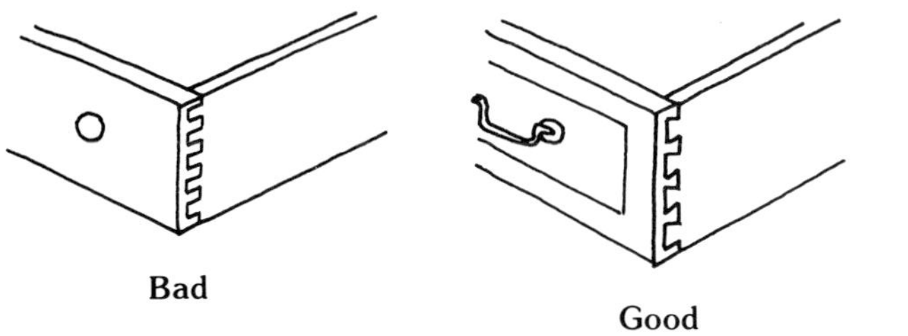

Dovetailed joints.

"Try on" a chair before making a purchase.

drawer bottoms from falling out as wood expands with heat and cold.

- To determine how well the drawers fit, pull one out about half way and move it from side to side. If it moves more than ¼ inch, it is not well made.
- Quality pieces have friction-free center drawer glides and dust-proof panels between drawers. Pull out a drawer and check these.
- Look at the back of chests. These should be securely screwed to the frame and well sanded and stained. There should also be a support fastened along the bottom.
- Be sure to examine hardware. Pulls and handles should be firmly attached, easy to grasp, and harmonious in styling.
- Look at the catch. A friction type catch wears out quickly. The magnetic type works better and is long lasting.

Judging Chair Quality

To judge chair quality, first, ask the manufacturer's name. If it is a familiar one it is more likely to be of good quality. Then check the wood. Tough woods, like oak, ash, birch, and hard maple should last a lifetime. Look at the frame. It should be glued and have corner blocks with screws and bolts—*never nails.* The upholstered seat should have fine-tempered springs wrapped in envelopes of resilient foam.

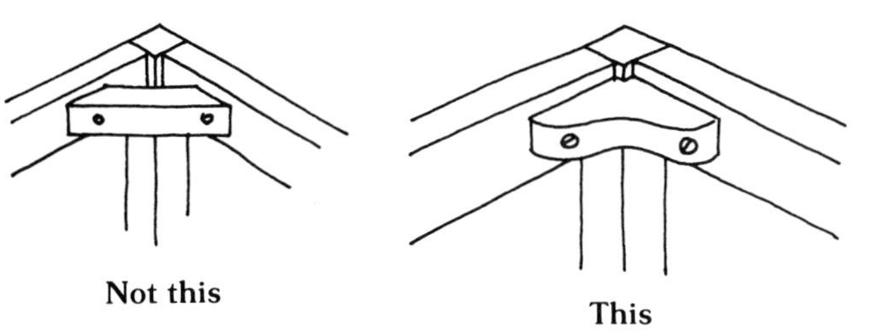

Chair leg support.

Buying Upholstered Furniture

When you buy upholstered furniture, use should determine your choice. Consider the fabric first, and then think about who will use it and where. After selecting the color, texture, and pattern of the fabric, ask about the durability of the fiber, surface finish, and ease of care.

Hidden under the cover of upholstered furniture is the cushioning or filling. New materials are being added continually, and older ones are being improved. It is difficult to keep up-to-date on all the new things, so ask meaningful questions: What kind of cushioning does the chair or sofa have? Is it soft, comfortable, and resilient? Will it retain its shape? Can it be cleaned? Is it odorless and allergy-free? Is it light enough to make the furniture easily movable?

The criterion for an upholstered chair or sofa should be comfort. No matter what the cost, the value to you is measured in terms of personal satisfaction. Here are some pointers to help you buy a chair:

- Avoid getting a chair that is too soft. The secret of comfort is not in the softness but in good support.
- A chair should be easy to get out of—try it.
- Be sure the arms are not too high. You need elbow room at a comfortable height.
- For relaxation, select an upholstered chair with a back high enough to support your back and rest your head. Avoid one with a scooped out back: it may cause strain on shoulder muscles.
- Avoid chairs with a soft seat and a high, hard edge. This can cause pain and swelling of the lower legs.
- The back of a chair should tilt backward slightly about 15 to 25 degrees for prolonged comfort.
- Avoid a chair that requires the sitter to jackknife at the hips or knees. This can cause muscle cramps.
- For a special person, buy a chair that fits. If you are buying a chair for another person, have that person try it on. Do the same for yourself.

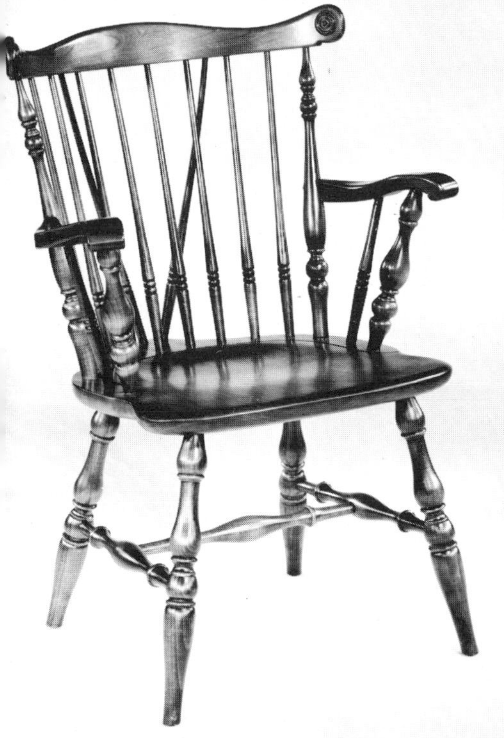

For Long Wear

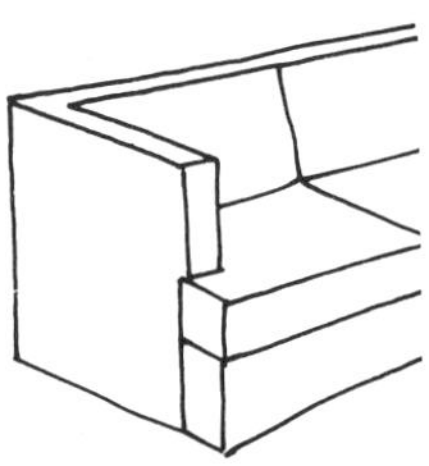

Do not choose this.

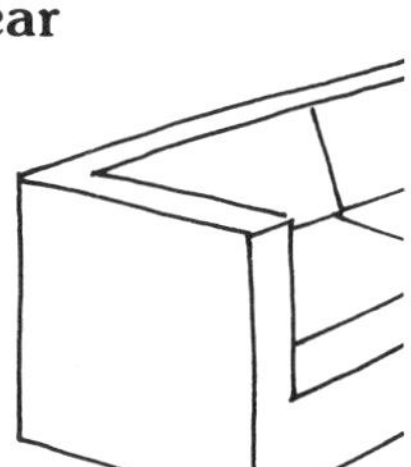

Choose this.

A slip seat is easy to replace.

- Get a chair that is in proportion to the other chairs in your room. It may be higher or lower, wider or narrower, but it mustn't overpower or be overpowered by the furnishings you already have.

To get the best service from your upholstered chairs and sofas, select those with loose cushions on the back and seat. They can be turned and used on both sides, thus doubling the life of the fabric. Also, select square seat cushions instead of T-shaped ones; the middle and end ones may be exchanged to increase the wear. Buy dining room chairs with slip seats that are easily removed and recovered. They take less material and wear longer, and recovering them is a simple matter.

It is wise to choose upholstered furniture that is basically plain, and not classified as belonging to any period. Such a piece, when covered with the right fabric, will fit into any decor you may have or may choose later on.

Because there are so many hidden values in furniture construction, it is important that you buy from a reputable dealer, and whenever possible choose brand names that you have seen advertised nationally. It cannot be emphasized strongly enough that you carefully read all manufacturers' tags on the furniture and check the guarantees.

Plastics for Furniture

Many furniture firms use plastic where they once used wood. See-through acrylic furniture is attractive and seems to occupy no space, but it scratches easily. Many molded plastic chairs and tables are of excellent design, are practical and durable, and come in a wide price range. The famous pedestal chair of Eero Saarinen, which has become a modern classic, will always be good. And it goes everywhere.

For some purposes, such as for tabletops that get hard usage, plastic may serve the purpose better and be more durable than wood. Vinyl (the term most often used for plastic surfaces) veneer has the look and feel of wood; needs no wax, stain, or varnish; resists scratches and most household liquids; and is easy to maintain. The veneer may be a vinyl laminate that actually contains a thin veneer of wood, or it may be either a vinyl that simulates wood graining through a photographic process or a veneer that is a combination of both.

Facing page: Three traditional chairs of great versatility and lasting beauty. Left: Windsor chair. *Courtesy of Ethan Allen.* Middle: French Provincial chair. *Courtesy of Drexel Heritage Furnishings.* Right: Queen Anne chair. *Courtesy of Ethan Allen. Below*: Three twentieth-century classics. Left: Bentwood chair by Hoffman. *Courtesy of Thonet.* Middle: Mies van der Rohe "Barcelona" chair. *Courtesy of Knoll International.* Right: Plastic pedestal chair by Eero Saarinen. *Courtesy of Knoll International.*

The gyro chair by Eero Aarino, sometimes called the "rock-and-roll." ***Courtesy of Stendig, Inc.***

Plastic on flat surfaces can be a practical and wise choice, but plastic simulating hand-carved pieces should be avoided: that smacks of pretense. Manufacturers refer to these pieces not as plastics but as vinyl veneers, high-pressure laminates, or molded components. Be familiar with man-made materials in furniture, and if they are used where they serve a definite function for you, they may be a better choice than wood.

Dual-Purpose Furniture

With living space at such a premium today, multipurpose furniture is needed more than ever before. Manufacturers have shown ingenious planning in creating pieces that serve a number of uses. Some such items are dining tables that double as desks, bars that are coffee tables, beds that store their own linen and bedding, desks that store chairs, sofas for conversation and sleeping, modular case goods with easy flexibility, and knock-down furniture that can be assembled at home.

Shopping Mass-Merchandise Stores

What of mass-merchandise stores? If you know how to recognize good furniture, you can usually find well-designed and well-constructed items in mass-merchandise stores. The main difference will be in the finish. Furniture that is mass produced may not be of the highest fashion; but this may be good, because high fashion is short lived, and high-fashion furniture is often faddish. Furniture with good design will never be dated.

Buying Furniture on Sale

January is usually the slow period in home-furnishing retail stores. Often you can make good purchases then, but your best guarantee of getting good furniture at discount prices is going to a reputable dealer.

What About Style?

Today's home and its furnishings are made up of a legacy from the past, plus design products of twentieth-century technology. Only recently have Americans begun to look to the past for inspiration to enhance their way of life. Along with the trend toward traditional architecture, there is a trend toward tradi-

The rural "English look" is shown here in beamed ceiling, sturdy oak furniture, diamond-paned windows, the colorful crewel embroidery, and the mellow pewter. The well-bred English look is evident in the carefully set table and the accessories throughout the room. *Courtesy of Ethan Allen.*

tional furniture, particularly among the young. They are searching long-neglected attics, used furniture stores, junk piles, and antique shops for discarded items that have a new appeal; things rooted in the past have taken on a special relevance in today's decorating. The Mediterranean craze that was carried to such extremes of bad taste in recent decades, has all but disappeared. The current demand is for simple, unpretentious, undated furniture.

What is your style preference? Are you familiar with the most common styles in use today? A thorough understanding of period styles of furniture is not necessary to create a charming home, but a knowledge of historical furnishings will deepen your aesthetic appreciation of your decorating heritage, broaden your concepts of interior design, and foster creative energies. A working knowledge of the most commonly used styles of furniture, both traditional and modern, will not only instill confidence in your own decorating ability, it will also provide a basis for intelligently deciding what is right for you and your family. It could possibly be the source of an exciting and continued interest.

An authentic interpretation of any specific style in today's home would be neither practical nor desirable. But to establish the *feeling* of a favorite period can provide lasting satisfaction.

Historic styles are many. Here we shall consider only those "adapted" styles in most common use today. They are in greatest demand because they meet the requirements of our twentieth-century way of living.

Before deciding on a style, consider carefully the general mood you wish to establish in your home. Do you want a homey, provincial atmosphere, or one that is more sophisticated but with a "lived-in" country look? Would you like graceful traditional, the nineteenth-century romantic look, sleek modern, or a comfortable informal mix? When you have determined the mood that reflects you and your household, you are ready to choose pieces that fit that mood.

Garrison

Informal Homey Provincial

For the informal look, the Early American is a favorite choice, especially for small houses. Early colonial architecture has been a favorite all across America since its inception in the seventeenth century. Its inherent charm, economy of construction, and its timeless design are never out of place. But because its beauty derives from its simplicity and symmetrical proportions, it must be handled expertly. Architects do not like to design houses of this general style because the façade does not "shout" to passersby. Early American architecture is quiet and unassuming, but when well handled, it reflects true and lasting quality.

Cape Cod

Salt box

Gambrel

Four types of seventeenth-century New England houses.

Early American is a much overworked label, and authors interpret it differently. When applied to home furnishings, it refers to a series of interpretations of European styles spanning roughly two hundred years. But when most people think "Early American" they conjure up the homey handcrafted look, a provincial look that is a potpourri of styles introduced and interpreted by the New England colonists of the seventeenth and early eighteenth centuries. More than any other style, it evokes in Americans a feeling of nostalgia, and it is one of the most enduring and livable styles.

To faithfully reproduce a seventeenth-century home today would be foolish; to capture the spirit and character of our ancestors' homes and still have the conveniences of the twentieth century is far more desirable.

For an Early American interior, floors with wide wood planks and braided or hooked rugs, or wall-to-wall carpet in shag or tweed would be appropriate.

Walls would be most authentic with one wall vertically paneled with molded edges (palisade wall) and other walls with rough plaster painted in a warm off-white, or covered with a quaintly patterned paper. There are many documentary patterns on the market. A dado with horizontal boards will give a genuine feeling of the period. Ceilings should be low, with plain plaster or with rough beams stained and waxed. A large fireplace opening with a picturesque hand-hewn lintel will give a

Early American

distinctive character to the room, but there are standard wood facings available. If you prefer, use a brick-faced opening with a raised hearth. Select fireplace accessories with care. Simple wrought-iron andirons with a gooseneck or a cannonball top will add just the right touch.

Windows should be simply treated. Unbleached muslin or a printed cotton with appropriate designs and colors would be suitable.

Furniture should be in natural wood, with a painted piece or two. Ladder-back chairs with rush-bottom seats, an open Welch cupboard, a trestle or gate-leg table, a spindle-armed sofa, a dough-box end table, and a cobbler's bench coffee table are some items of furniture that will give your room the Early American flavor.

Colors are typically warm and earthy with deep, rich blue and red. Fabrics, always of prime importance, should have rugged textures and quaint designs to reflect the homespun look.

Accessories, those important little things in setting the mood, are virtually unlimited. Select such things as a wag-on-the-wall clock, primitive folk art, gaily decorated tole, a few pieces of pewter, a decoy, and a piece of hobnail and pressed glass. Lamps, always a major item, can be many things. Use such bases as a hitching post, a small milk can, or a lantern, with simple off-white shades made of handcrafted-looking fabric. For a chandelier, the New Bedford Whaler, or a wagon-wheel style would carry out the mood.

The Country Look

In recent years, the so-called country look is filling the needs of many people. Whether the name is "Rural English," the "Well-bred English look," or "Country French," the current country look is unpretentious but has an unmistakable air of sophistication and a genuine character and quality that reflects use and care.

The exterior of a house with the country look may be an adaptation of either English half-timber, commonly called "Tudor," or French seventeenth-century. The interior of both may have much the same feeling, which is a cloistered one—dark wood floors with oriental or richly colored rugs, beamed ceilings, walls that are paneled, papered, or covered with fabric.

If the Country French look is your favorite, use fabrics profusely, combining florals and plaids. The surest way to say "Country French" is to let a toile de Jouy establish your living room or bedroom. Put the print on the walls, at the windows, and on one or more pieces of furniture. Choose salamander-back side chairs, a French-style wing chair, and a Louis XV style bureau plat. An armoire would be a great purchase. Hang a panetière (a bread cooler) on the wall, and select a very French clock. These will give your room the unmistakable feeling of "Country French." Combine all or some of these with furniture you already have. If your upholstered pieces need recovering, select appropriate fabrics. Replacing hardware on old pieces may add a further note of authenticity.

French Manor

Country French

If the "well-bred English look" (from rural England) is your choice, backgrounds should have some architectural interest from the half-timber style or the small panels of the early seventeenth century. Floors should be dark wood planks with oriental rugs or rich-toned area rugs. Rooms done in this mood have a quality of lived-in opulence with a svelte masculinity. Windows with diamond panes and a fireplace with Tudor arch will add authenticity. Much of the beauty of this look is in the furniture; it combines a robust structure with a mellow finish. The look is varied and versatile and understandably so—it spans centuries of history, ranging from Gothic to Regency. A trestle table, a Restoration chair, heavy nested tables, and a comfortable sofa covered with crewel embroidery, will help set the mood.

A handsome period clock, a globe table, and a coat of arms will add further to the genuine English feeling. Colors should be rich primaries. Fabrics should consist

The homey country look here is expressed in the overhead beams, rugged furniture, colorful printed fabric, and invitingly arranged furniture. The pottery, tin, and pewter add to the total feeling of provincial charm. *Courtesy of Armstrong Cork Co.*

of blocked linens, chintzes, crewel embroidery, velvets, and tweeds. This style of decorating provides an environment for good living and promises to be with us indefinitely.

The Formal Traditional Look

When we hear "traditional" applied to interior furnishings, we tend to think of the graceful furniture and decorative arts of England during the eighteenth century. Actually, though, the term *traditional* may refer to furnishings of any country so long as it is one of the more formal styles.

Eighteenth-Century France. From eighteenth-century France we get the excessively ornate rococo of Louis XV and the elegantly delicate neoclassic of Louis XVI. Excellent reproductions of these sumptuous styles are being made today, and the feeling is very much alive. Sometimes it has a surprising authenticity, and as a result it is always in demand among a wealthy clientele. But because this elegant, formal furniture is not appropriate for most American families, the furniture of the Louis XV period has been simplified to produce an extremely popular and versatile style that Americans have termed *French Provincial.* Although most Americans have preferred to use French Provincial in a rather formal setting, it may be successfully dressed down. The choice of fabric will determine the degree of formality. Accessories here may be as elegant as personal taste dictates. French Provincial is an ideal setting for those who want casual comfort with an air of elegance. (See page 63.)

The neoclassic style of Louis XVI has been the choice of Americans who love delicate elegance. This basic style has been simplified for American use and is termed *Italian Provincial.* It is characterized by digni-

Tudor half-timber

Rural English

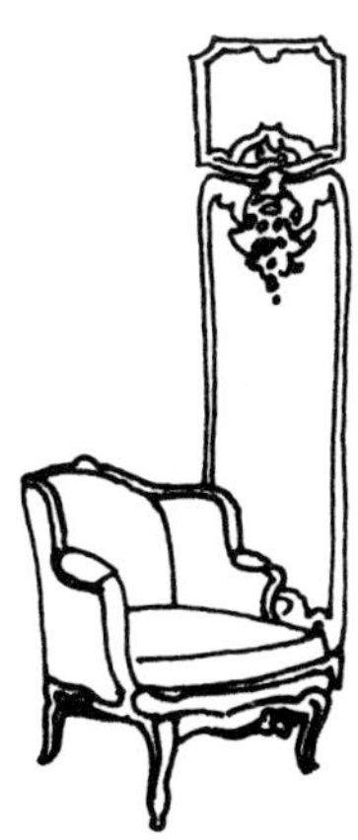

Louis XV

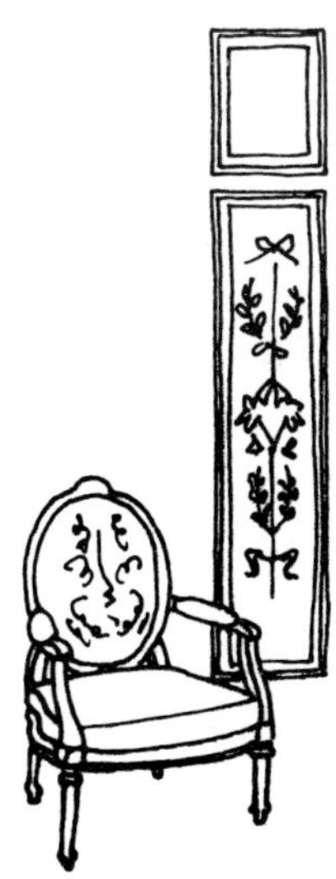

Louis XVI

The spirit of the past is recaptured in this comfortable living room. The wide hearth with its deep lintel and authentic early accessories, the rag rug, crewel drapery, and documentary fabric on the sofa arouse a feeling of nostalgia in many people. We call this look Early American. *Courtesy of Ethan Allen.*

fied simplicity that creates a mood of restrained elegance. With this furniture, select soft colors (green, gold, venetian blue, and white) and the stripes and classic designs of late eighteenth-century France and Italy. Use damasks, brocatelles, and cut velvets. Formal paneling, architectural paper, Japanese grass cloth, or flocked paper in classic designs is appropriate for walls. Plain-weave wall-to-wall carpeting, Aubusson, or Savonnerie rugs, or faded Orientals are good for both French and Italian Provincial. (See page 74.)

Eighteenth-Century England. The English furnishings of the eighteenth century have a different feeling from the French of the same period. Early in the century, furniture in the Queen Anne style assumed a comfort, grace, and charm hitherto unknown in England. The great cabinetmakers of the "Golden Age," notably Chippendale, Hepplewhite, Sheraton, and the Brothers Adam, reached a perfection that has never been surpassed. The dignity and refinement of these styles, which are known as "Georgian," had great appeal to

Georgian

Americans of that day and have continuously been a favorite with many discriminating people. Reproductions and adaptations of eighteenth-century English furniture are again in the forefront of all leading furniture lines in America today. People of all ages are enthusiastically responding to the grace and charm of the Georgian style, setting a new mood in their homes or mixing it with what they have.

To create the traditional look of eighteenth century England and America, walls should have molded paneling with cornice and dado or should be papered with a documentary design. Floors may be hardwood with oriental rugs or wall-to-wall carpet in a plain weave.

Windows may be draped with damask or antique satin and topped by a shaped cornice covered in the same fabric.

The fireplace facing may be marble with bolection molding. Authentically designed milled work such as fireplace facings, doors, windows, and stairways are available in good supply.

Seldom would one want to have every piece of furniture in the same style, but it is necessary to have a number of pieces to establish the Georgian feeling. A wing chair in the Queen Anne or Chippendale style is a must. A breakfront, a camel-back sofa, and a Queen Anne tea table, or a piecrust tile-top table will add a feeling of dignity.

Many manufacturers are producing reproductions of English eighteenth-century furniture today, but some items of authentic traditional furniture can also be purchased in easy-to-assemble, money-saving kits. Using these kits, even the do-it-yourselfer with little skill can create authentic, charming reproductions.

Colors for this style are rich reds, blues, greens, and gold. Fabrics may be damask, velvets, brocades, and leather. For a less formal look, printed cottons in suitable patterns are appropriate. The choice of fabric is the key to achieving the degree of formality or informality desired.

Although Georgian tends to be formal, it is a good mixer. This timeless decorating style can be adapted in fresh new ways to bring it in tune with today's needs and still retain the charm, beauty, and grace of the past. The best of the past and the best of the present will always be compatible. But, traditional requires an honesty of materials. Plastic imitations have no place here. (See page 45.)

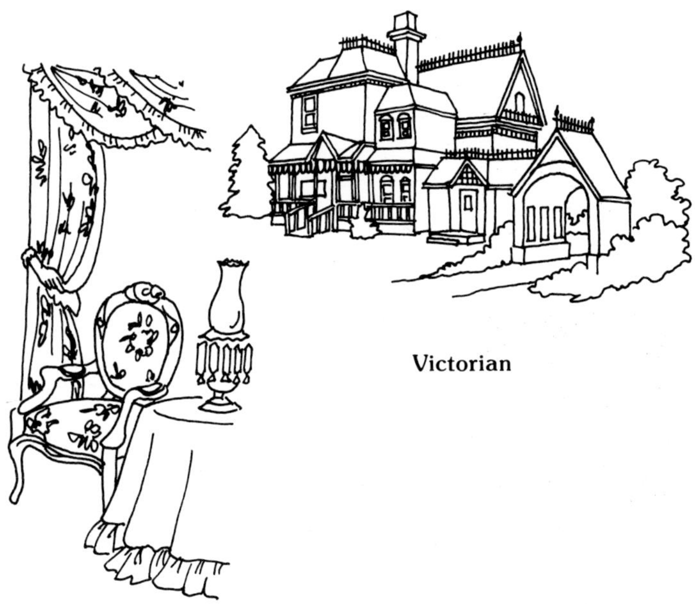

Victorian

Romantic Victorian

Furniture of the nineteenth century, which a few years ago was regarded as pure junk, today is being sought after as prized antiques. After moving from parlor to attic to junk yard to antique shop, Victorian furniture is again back in the living room, and many of its admirers are enthusiastically refinishing it and putting it to work.

During the sixty-four years that Queen Victoria sat upon the throne of England, styles from Gothic

What could be a more cheerful spot for a gathering of friends than this Victorian corner? Wicker chairs, floor-length table cover, floral wallpaper and fresh flowers. *Courtesy of Collins and Aikman.*

through Empire were revived in America, often combined without regard to compatibility of style or pattern. Although Victorian can be many things, the image most commonly evoked is the lavish Belter parlor with its floral wallpaper and floral carpet; one or more ornately carved "suites" consisting of a love seat, two or three tables and a lady's and a gentleman's chairs upholstered in red velvet; a generous supply of fancy chairs, beribboned and fringed; several whatnots laden with collections of things; dried flowers under glass domes; and an oval fireplace opening topped by a mantel overcrowded with rococo ornaments.

This is the old stereotype; Victorian today is greatly moderated. Mixed with modern, the result can provide the best of two worlds, as many people, young and old, have discovered.

Modern

At any time in history when a new art form emerges that breaks all ties with previous design forms—whether it is in music, architecture, or furniture—it is referred to as *modern*. In each era it has been an expression of the times. Today modern furniture design is an expression of the twentieth century, and it aptly suggests the tempo of modern Americans. The key word in modern design is "functionalism." Function determines the form of each object, with an emphasis on line, proportion, color, texture, and finish.

Common features are simplicity of planes and surfaces and the use of plastics, metals, and glass. Molded plastic chairs are sturdy, light, durable, and relatively inexpensive. Plastic-laminated surfaces are impervious to moisture, may simulate natural wood

A console table can serve many purposes. *Below*: Natural grain wood with oriental feeling could go in any decor. *Courtesy of The Lane Company, Inc. Right*: Beautiful modern chrome and glass would enhance most rooms. *Courtesy of The Lane Company, Inc.*

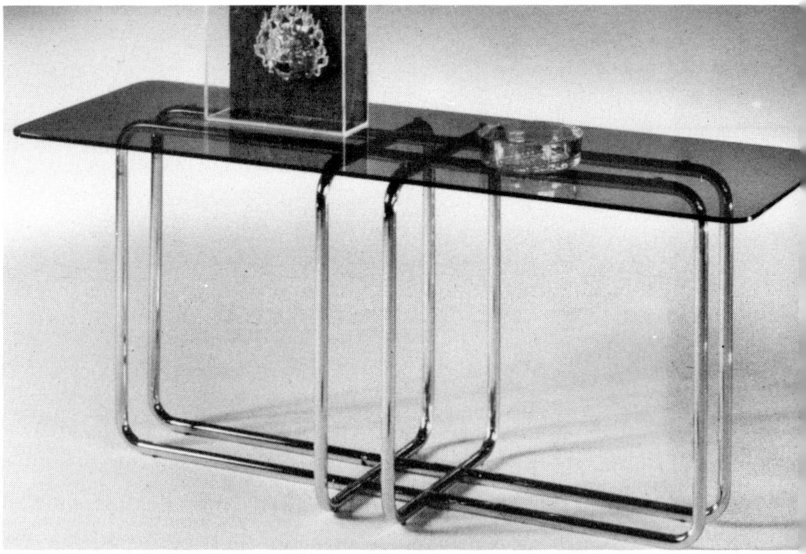

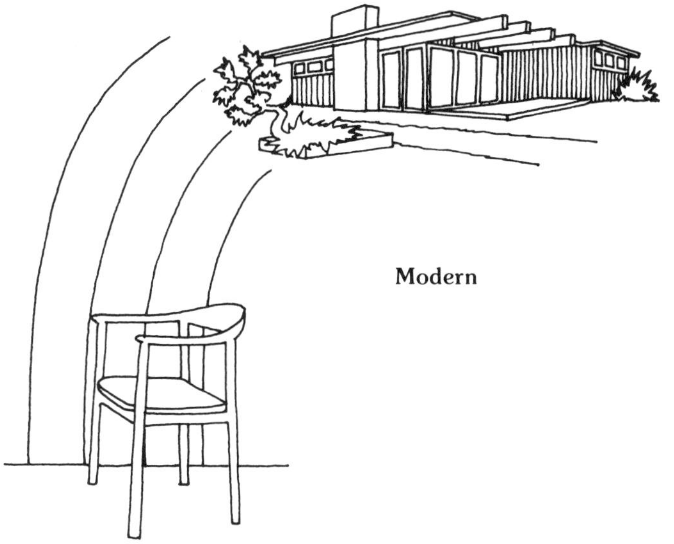

Modern

grains, and are easy to maintain. The new, inflatable plastic furniture is practical for Americans on the move and when in use, it seems to float, making it a good choice for rooms with limited space. Items of brass and steel combined with wood are popular.

Modern is many things. It is sleek and functional, puffy and comfortable, formal and informal, expensive or priced to fit the most modest budget. Modern is stimulating, youthful, flexible, and easy to care for.

Backgrounds may be sleek, dramatically papered, or strongly architectural. Woods are left in the most natural state. Fabrics emphasize texture for contrast, with vinyls playing an important role. Pattern is bold, in abstract or conventional designs with motifs drawn from any source. Color schemes from sophisticated white, silver, or neutral monochromatics to sharp contrasts in unusual combinations are suitable. Carpets range from long-haired animal skins to Orientals. Personal choice alone will limit the hard floor coverings.

Choose modern furniture with an eye to good design. New advances in technology are bringing about frequent changes in materials and methods of production which make modern furniture vulnerable to a sudden turn in fashion.

Since the early twentieth century, modern has gone through many stages, each contributing something of lasting value. Some of the best-known furniture designs, which have become twentieth-century classic, are Mies van der Rohe's Barcelona chair (which has a timeless elegance), Michael Thonet's well-known bentwood chair, Hans Wegener's "The Chair," Charles Eames's famous molded rosewood chairs, and Eero Saarinen's much-copied molded-plastic pedestal chair. Any one of these would add an air of distinction to a room and should be familiar to every alert American.

Mixing Styles

Today, very few people buy matched items of furniture (as was once customary), nor do they maintain the same style of furniture throughout the house or even throughout the same room. The eclectic look is the thing—a mixing rather than a matching. The one-of-a-kind look is the one most preferred. But eclectic does not mean a hodgepodge. Pieces must be related in scale and chosen with a final goal in mind. Success will be more surely achieved if there is a common theme running through your entire scheme—some element

Right: **Well-designed, sturdy furniture lined against the wall, and a pull-out bed for an overnight guest make the best use of space in this small room. Ample storage and display space for personal belongings placed against rich warm colors helps to create a handsome retreat.** ***Courtesy of Drexel Heritage Furnishings.***

Eclectic

tying the whole together. For example, to achieve the provincial look, informality is the key; and all country furniture, regardless of the source, is compatible. For the traditional look, dignity is the key, and refined pieces of almost any style can be combined together with happy result. For the modern look, be a bit daring and imaginative.

Whatever the general theme of a room, it ought not to be so dominant that it creates a feeling of monotony. Interest can often be brought into a room by the unexpected. For example, a pair of Victorian chairs placed in a modern setting will do something very special to the room. A modern sofa will give a period room a fresh up-dated look. An up-to-date arrangement of traditional furniture can reemphasize its beauty. The clean sweep of modern decor may serve as the most effective background for a highly prized antique. Today, more than ever before, people are taking a more mature look at furnishings of the past and the present, and they are finding new ways to use them. In furnishings of the past, we are finding much that can be borrowed to enrich present-day living, and from the present there is much that can add new life to the old. As new foreign influences come along, each can be adapted to enhance our lives and meet present-day needs without discarding everything from yesterday. In this way we are developing a more mature way of decorating our homes.

It is easy to shop for coordinated furniture, but a room decorated this way is lacking in interest. The well-done eclectic interior shows more sophistication and infinitely more discrimination. If you have a turn-of-the-century house and want modern furnishings, don't hesitate. Do just that! If your house is modern, but you have always hankered for a suite of Belter furniture, get one! The juxtaposition of a Victorian antique against hard-edge modern may create the unexpected that will delight you.

When selecting furniture, do not be too concerned with style names. Use them only as guidelines. Find out what features distinguish one style from another, what mood is created by each, and which styles can and which cannot be compatibly used together. Learn what constitutes a genuine antique, a reproduction, and an adaptation. Use the library. Read a variety of good magazines. Examine model rooms in stores. Pay particular attention to homes you like. These will enable you to shop with more discrimination and get the best value for your money.

Too many people today are buying elaborate furniture because they mistakenly think it looks expensive. They are influenced by the fact that the percentage of bad household furnishings available is far too high.

To be an intelligent shopper, you should become familiar with the style names of the most commonly used pieces of furniture. Certain identifying names have been given to different styles of furniture; and although details such as legs, arms, and backs will vary widely, the general shapes can be easily recognized.

- Upholstered chairs and sofas are identified by their general shape, height from the floor, types of backs, arms, and legs. Although some details such as cushion treatment and trim will vary with the individual designer, they can usually be identified.
- Many different kinds of tables are used today. Decorative details such as legs, feet, and points of design will vary according to the style of the period, but the general characteristics remain the same and can be recognized.
- Case furniture is a general term for pieces of furniture used for holding things. In cabinet work it refers to the shell of a piece of furniture, such as a chest of drawers, or any type of cabinet. As with chairs and tables, the details in case pieces will differ depending upon the period design, but the major characteristics remain the same. (See pages 96–97.)

Furniture Identification

Furniture Identification

12 Comfortably Seated

Is furniture arrangement a problem for you? It is for most people. Usually the main problem is the room itself. If rooms were well proportioned and if doors and windows were placed with furniture in mind, most problems could be avoided. Too often, houses are planned from the outside to conform to the architect's design and if the client does not clearly specify definite requirements for wall space, the result too often is rooms that are almost impossible to arrange for comfort and convenience.

The key word in today's furniture arrangement, for every room, is *efficiency*. Strict adherence to any set of rules will most likely be inappropriate. When arranging furniture in any room in your home, you should give first priority to your family and your way of life. How will the room be used? Beauty and good design are important, but comfort and convenience are the most essential. It is possible for a room to be pleasant in appearance but impractical for living.

In spite of the differences in the way people live, certain guidelines in the arrangement of furniture should provide some help.

Guidelines for Arranging Furniture

- Plan each room with purpose in mind. Decide what the room will be used for and by whom.
- Use furniture that is in keeping with the scale of the room. The overall dimensions and the architectural background should determine the size and general feeling of the furnishings.
- Provide space for traffic. Doorways should be free. Major traffic lanes must be unobstructed. It is sometimes necessary to redirect traffic in a room; this can be accomplished by skillful furniture placement and by the use of screens and dividers.
- Arrange furnishings to give the room a sense of equilibrium. Opposite walls should seem the same so that the room will be at rest. Where neither archi-

Comfort is the key in this restful atmosphere. Warm earthy tones, simplicity of line, adequate light, and plenty of space to put things down in this well-arranged grouping invite one to sit and linger. *Courtesy of Drexel Heritage Furnishings.*

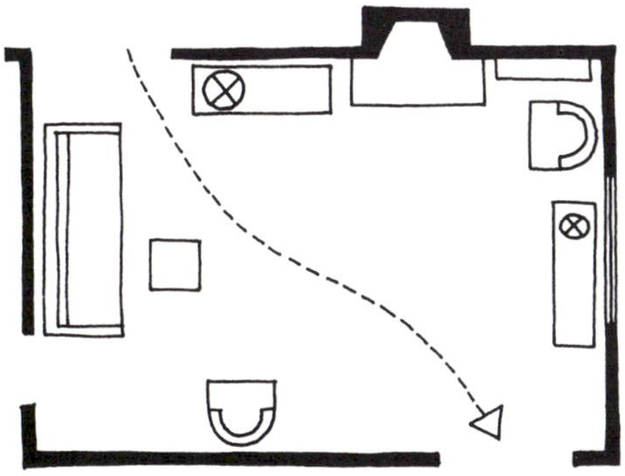

Traffic lane divides the room.

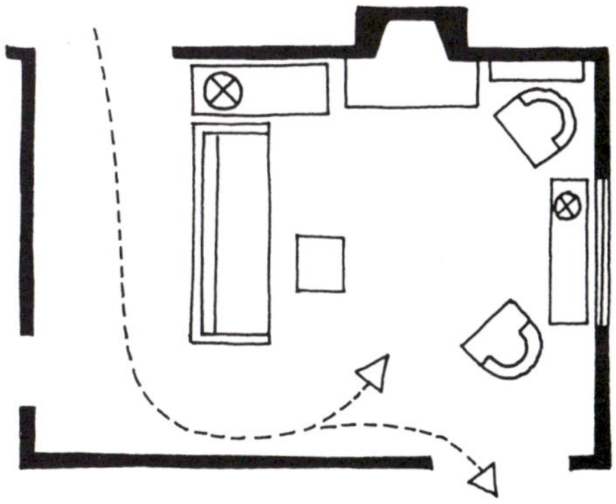

Redirecting the traffic restricts the conversation area.

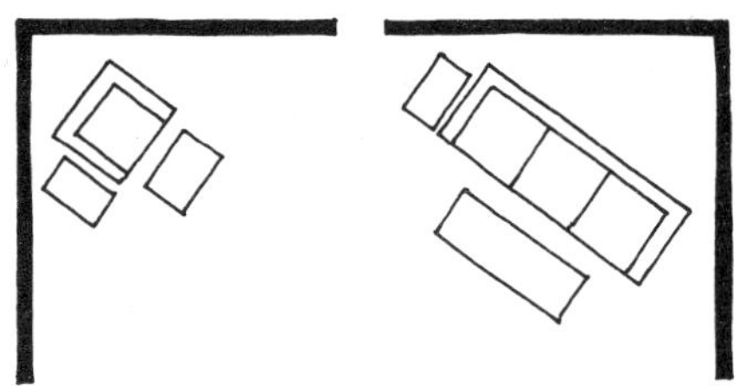

A heavy lounge chair is often better across a corner, but do not cross a corner with a large piece of furniture.

In a room with a slanted ceiling, the heaviest furniture grouping should be against the highest wall.

tectural features nor furniture distribution can create this feeling, it may be achieved through the knowledgeable use of color, fabrics, and accessories.

- Achieve a good balance of high and low, angular and rounded furniture. Where furniture is all or predominantly low, the feeling of height may be created by incorporating shelves, mirrors, pictures, and hangings into a grouping.
- Consider architectural and mechanical features. There should be no interference with the opening of windows or swinging of doors, or with heating or air-conditioning devices. Lamps should be placed near electrical outlets.
- Do not overcrowd a room. It is always better to be underfurnished than overfurnished. Some empty space between groupings helps to give an uncluttered effect. An occasional open space or empty corner may enhance a room and give the occupants breathing space. On the other hand, a room may be too stark and uninviting. Avoid either extreme.
- Large pieces of furniture should be placed parallel to the walls. Crossing a corner with a sofa or a case piece gives a room a disturbing feeling. On the other hand, a heavy lounge chair may be more pleasing when placed at an angle, since a large chair at right angles often feels stiff and unfriendly.
- Avoid pushing large pieces tightly into a corner, or touching floor-to-ceiling windows where a passageway should be allowed.
- Arrange the heaviest furniture grouping along the higher wall in rooms with slanted ceilings.
- Group furniture according to function. Rarely is a piece of furniture complete in itself; it calls for related pieces for function, comfort, or both. For example, a desk needs a chair; a piano needs a bench; a lounge chair and sofa need a table. Most groupings need lighting, so choose the appropriate lamp or lighting to provide adequate light. Last is the placement of the small accessories that provide the personal touch to the room.
- Allow space for people. Rooms are for people to live in and enjoy. Remember that they need leg room when sitting and space for getting up and moving about. The space within a group should be less than the distance between individual groups. Avoid a spotty appearance.

Furnishing Rooms of Various Shapes

If a room is well proportioned and the openings conveniently located to allow adequate wall space, furniture arrangement seldom presents a problem. But, rooms that are square or long and narrow require special treatment.

- The *square room* or the room that is nearly square has the least pleasing proportions. To alter the vis-

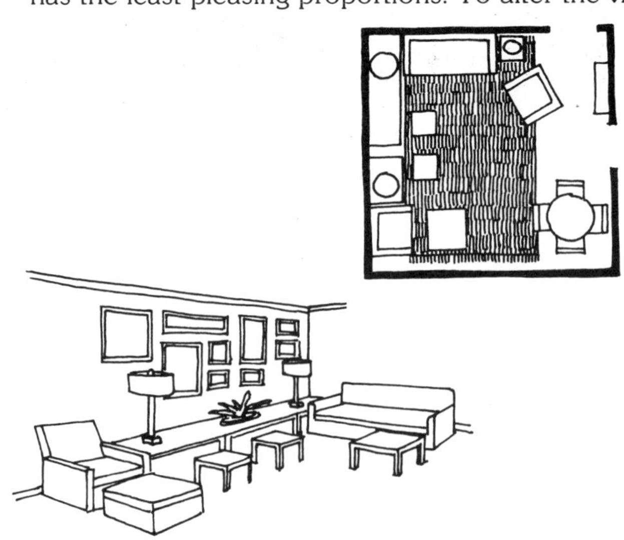

Skillfully planned furniture arrangements change the apparent proportions of a square room.

Well planned, comfortable, and uncluttered, this long room shows a well-balanced arrangement of furniture for eating and conversation. The deep shag rug is a nice contrast against the unglazed quarry tile floor. Plants offset the hard-edged undraped windows. *Courtesy of American Olean Tile Co.*

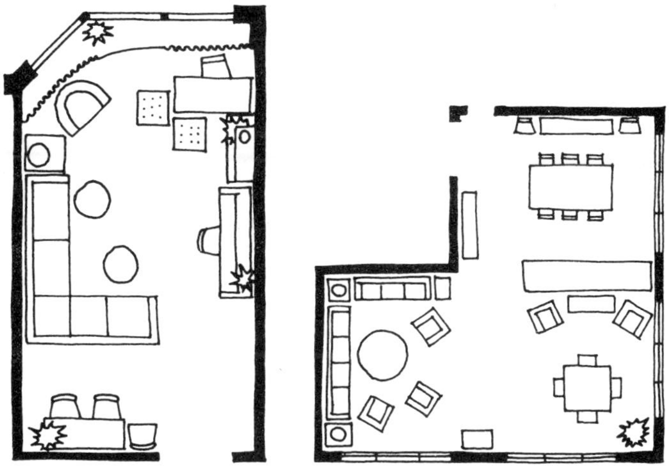

Left: Principles of optical illusion alter the apparent proportions of a long, narrow room. The curved line of drapery, the angled sofa, and the desk placed at a right angle to the long wall make the room seem wider. *Right*: A divider provides storage and privacy in an L-shaped room.

ual dimensions, you will need to use the principles and elements of design. For example, choose an area rug the full length of the room, but less than the width, and lay it near one long side, leaving a walkway. Arrange the furniture to create a rectangular effect. Remember what color can do.

- The *long, narrow room* may present a problem, but a knowing use of a few principles of optical illusion can visually modify the actual proportions. First, you must determine the activity centers. Then, if you wish to maintain the visual appearance of one large, flexible room, keep the furniture that stands out from the wall low. If you wish to make separate compartments, use some high pieces as dividers. Place furniture at right angles to the long wall to cut the length. Sectional furniture may turn a corner to create a cross-room grouping. Use rugs to define areas, preferably placing them at right angles to the long wall. Employ dividers and screens to divide activity centers that cut the length. Hang ceiling fixtures low to draw groupings together. Always let color work for you.
- The *L-shaped room* lends itself naturally to a division of activities, particularly living and dining. Area rugs, dividers, and furniture placement can easily create livable space in this shaped room.
- A *room with a jog* need not be a problem. Utilize the offset area in such a way that it becomes a feature of, and a real asset to, the room.

Furniture Arrangement for Specific Rooms

Each room of the house presents a unique problem according to its function; and since the functions of different rooms may vary greatly, each one must be considered separately.

Entrance Hall

An entry is a passageway and should not be cluttered. Empty space permitting an easy flow of traffic is essential. The size of the room will necessarily determine the amount and scale of the furniture that must be placed against the wall.

Living Room

The conversation area is the most important group in the living room. The main thing to keep in mind when planning this area is that its function is to provide an intimate grouping, out of the line of traffic, in which people can hear and be heard in a relaxed atmosphere. The optimum distance across this area is about eight feet, but plans should be made for converting this into a large group by including occasional chairs that have been located at convenient points. Built-in seating is not usually so comfortable nor so

Modular units have numerous possibilities. Here five armless chairs, two corner units, one ottoman, and an ottoman table create an area of repose. The console table provides a necessary surface. *Courtesy of Thayer Coggin, Inc.*

flexible as sofas and chairs that may be regrouped for more intimate occasions or that are opened out to invite more participants. Move-about modular furniture is the answer to having a flexible arrangement. You may start out by getting two or three separate pieces that fit together and can be added to later on. Six basic conversation groups can be arranged with modular furniture—depending on your space and your pocket book.

- The straight-line group is ideal for public places, but is not conducive to intimate conversation.

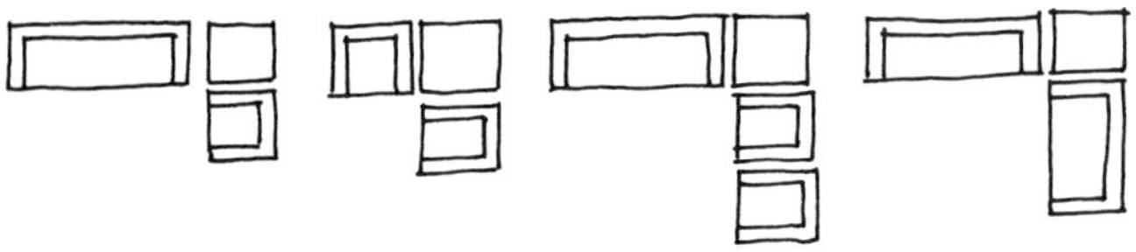

- The L-shape group is good for conversation and lends itself to either small or large areas.

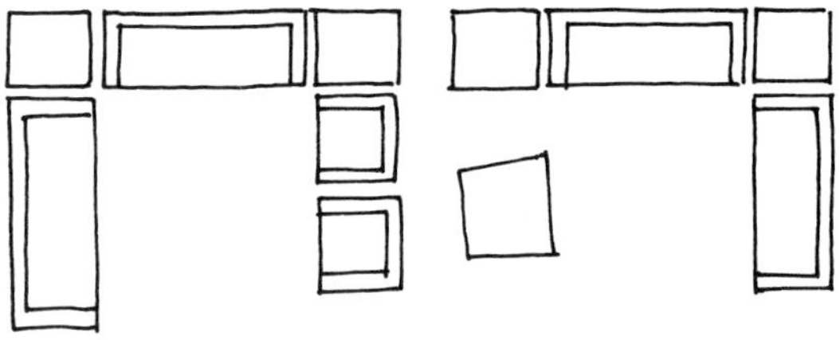

- The U-shape group is comfortable and attractive but requires more space.

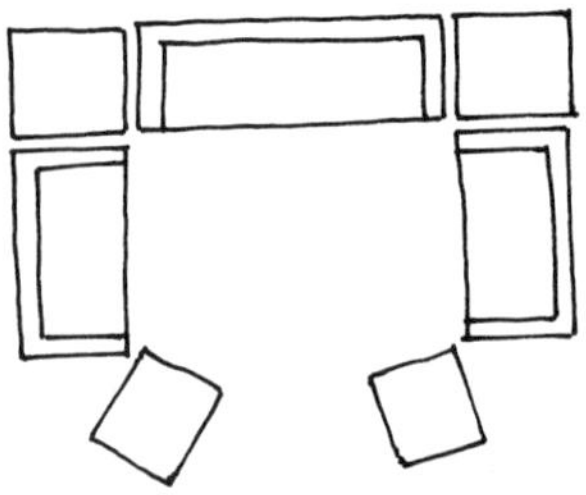

- The box-shaped group is one of the best, but allowances must be made for opening it to present a friendly appearance.

Fun and functional. Here a "Bunker Hill" effect is created with movable modular geometrics covered with nubby loop carpet and enlivened by colorful cushions. This area has a youthful appeal. *Courtesy of Colonnade Carpets and Collins and Aikman Co.*

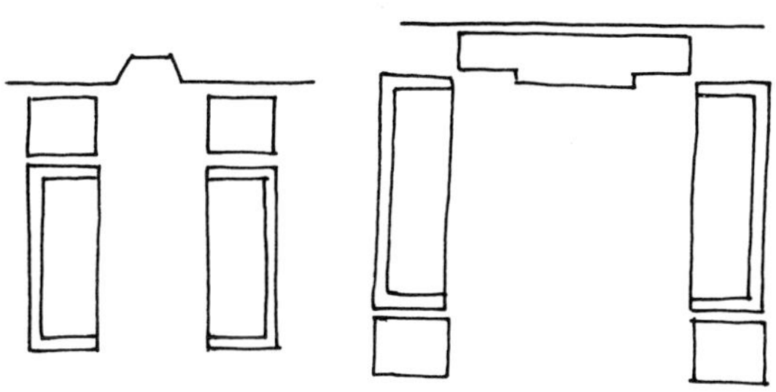

- The parallel grouping emphasizes an existing focal point such as a fireplace, or helps in creating a focal point such as a wall grouping.

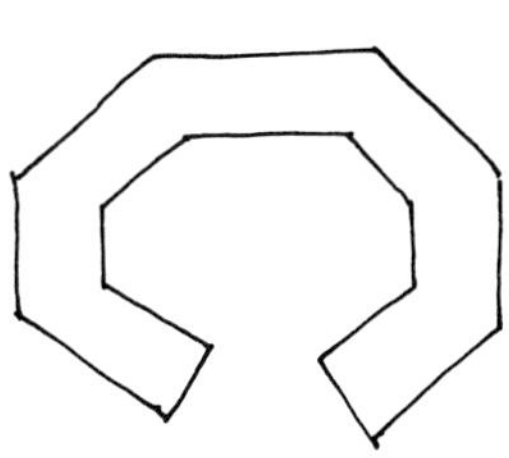

- The circular grouping can encompass an entire room if the room is small. A focal point can be created with modular units, or they may be used for a sunken built-in. The sunken conversation pit has found favor particularly with young people, but it is restrictive. It serves well as a supplementary area where space will allow, but it is not usually preferred for the principal conversation area of a living room.

Soft lighting gives a feeling of intimacy to conversation, but this does not mean semidarkness. People need to see the features of those with whom they are talking. A low-hanging light can pull a grouping together and may serve for reading when turned to its maximum power. It is advisable to avoid hanging mirrors where people talking can look up and see themselves. This is distracting and can be very annoying.

Chairs in the living room should be comfortable and not all the same type or size. Since people are built differently, what is comfortable for one person may be uncomfortable for another. Chairs should not be rigidly placed. This can give a guest the uneasy feeling that to alter the placement may be a major calamity. Don't place a wing chair where it obstructs a view or turns its back toward anyone entering the room. Near each lounge chair and sofa, the right table should be conveniently placed to hold a lamp and small items such as books, magazines, and light refreshments.

A pair placed side by side.

A pair in a corner for privacy.

The use of pairs has returned together with the traditional influence in today's furnishings. Identical pairs such as love seats, chairs, and lamps can be a unifying factor and hence a real asset to a room. But there is danger in using too many pairs. The result may be a room with monotony and lacking in interest.

Finding the right wall space for a piano is often a problem, but an upright piano need not stand against a wall. Try placing it at right angles to a wall, with a low screen behind it. The screen will serve as a background for a small chair and table. If the piano is low, back it up to a sofa, thus providing a convenient surface for a lamp, and the pianist can then face the room. A vertical piano may also serve as a room divider. Dress up the back with a piece of fabric that blends with the room.

The grand piano may be more difficult to place in the average room because of its size and because the straight side should in most cases be parallel to the wall. A bay window furnishes a beautiful setting for a grand piano, but the changes of temperature are hard on the instrument. In a dual-purpose room a grand piano may be placed to form a room divider. Whatever the location, the performer should face into the room.

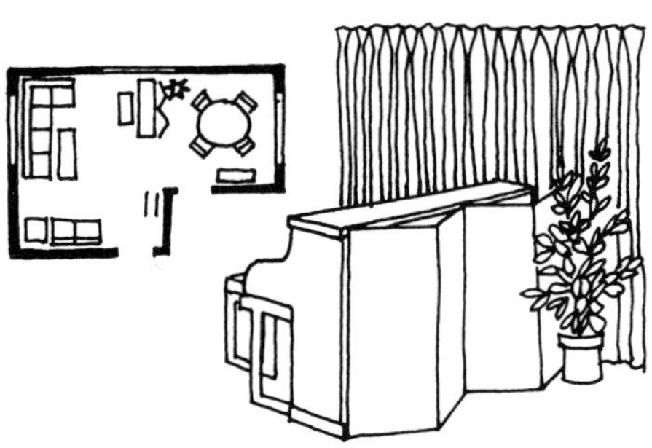

An upright piano serves as a partial room divider.

The flat side of the piano should be parallel to the wall.

In the living room most tables should be used only where there is a functional need. The scale, shape, and height of each table must be right for the purpose and size of the chair or sofa it accompanies. Console ta-

Living Room 14' × 24' Four Arrangements

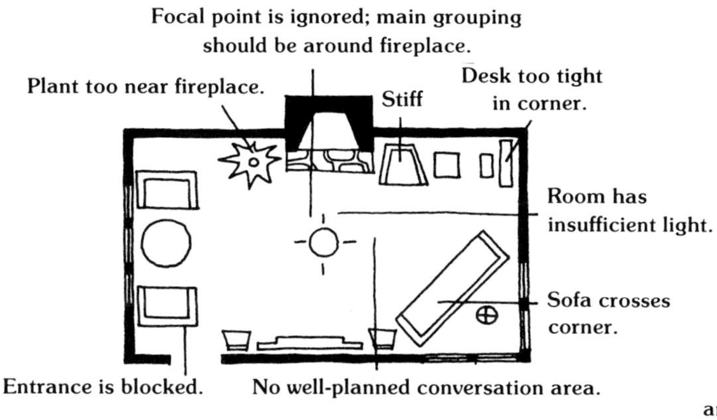

Poor arrangement

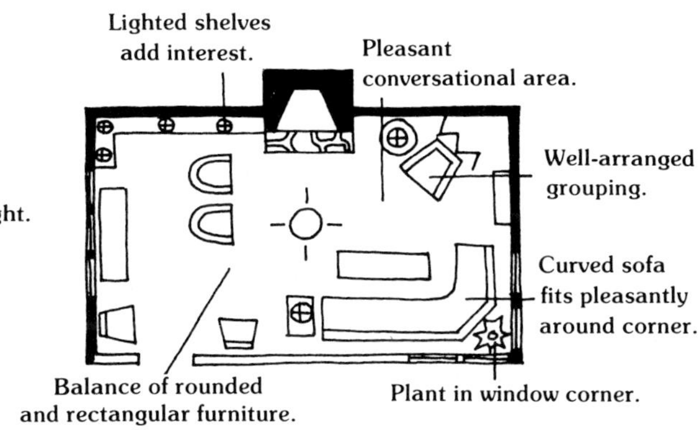

Good arrangement

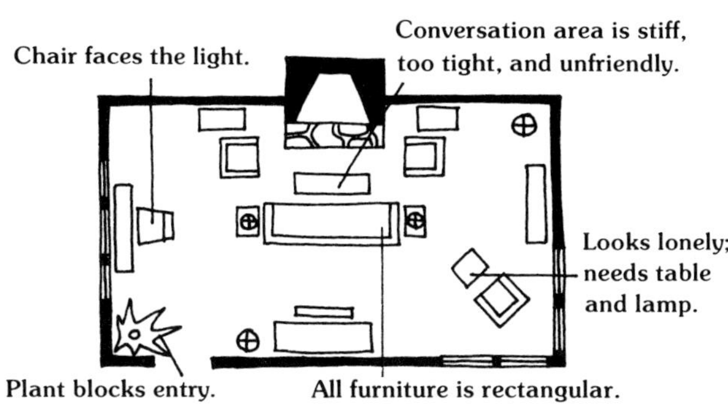

Poor arrangement

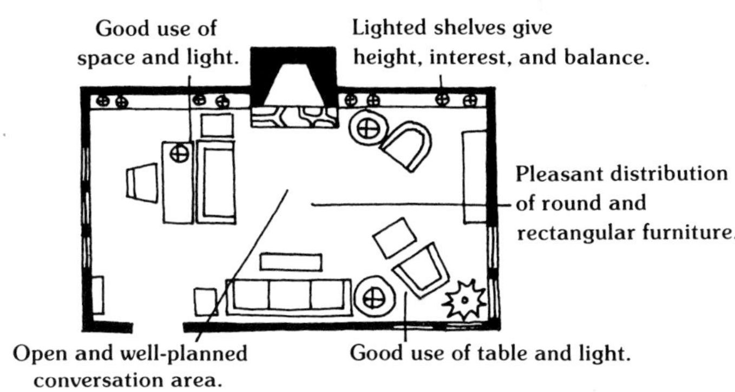

Good arrangement

bles can be decorative as well as functional and, when combined with a mirror or picture, are an asset to almost any room. The game table is usually collapsible, but where a permanent one is used, it may serve other purposes, such as for study or for snacks. The writing-table-desk gives a room a lived-in appearance and may also serve a dual purpose. Placed with its short side to the wall near a window or as part of a wall of books, it is convenient and usually contributes more to the general attractiveness of the room than when pushed flat against a wall. When the desk is placed in front of a window, the chair should be placed behind it, facing away from the light.

Large case or storage pieces should be located in convenient places and should be placed to give the room a feeling of balance. They should be centered if the area is small and balanced by other furniture where wall space is ample. Examine the four arrangements in the living room above.

The Dining Room

The dining room seldom affords much variety in furniture arrangement. Usually the table is placed in the center of the room with a chest or buffet for storage against the longest wall and a small serving piece near the kitchen door. If the room is large enough, a high piece such as a breakfront or a china cabinet can provide space for display (and add dignity as well). Corner cupboards are often the answer for storage and display in smaller rooms. Select chairs that are not too wide across the front. The extra width is unnecessary and takes up too much room around the table. Where space is limited, a round or oval table will allow more room for passage and will seat people more easily than a rectangular table of the same width and length.

Starting upper left and running clockwise. An island bed, easily assembled for box springs and mattress or for mattress alone. A panel bed and night stands are congenial companions. A pair of armoires with connecting canopy and vanity shelf. Armoires and canopy combine with bed. *Courtesy of Henredon Furniture Industries, Inc.*

If the dining area is small, it may be advisable to use a dropleaf table that may be closed and placed against the wall when not in use. A wall-hung shelf can serve in lieu of a buffet.

In planning the dining room, remember that people need space. To get into a chair at the table requires about two feet. For one person to assist in seating another requires about four-and-a-half-feet.

Family and Recreation Rooms

In most homes the family room and the recreation room are combined. Space does not usually permit two separate areas for informal living. Here more than any other areas of the house, the arrangement of furniture should be flexible to permit easy adjustment for various activities. Use, convenience, and practicability should be the guiding principles in arranging furniture in these rooms.

Bedrooms

There is usually less choice in the arrangement of furniture in a bedroom than in other rooms; therefore, carefully planned space is especially important. Before furniture arrangement begins, decide upon the purposes the room will serve in addition to sleeping. Because of its size, the bed will occupy the dominant place in the room, and seldom is there more than one wall large enough to accommodate it. Once the bed is established, traffic lanes should be planned, with careful attention given to nighttime walking. The foot of the bed is often a good place for a storage chest or a narrow bench. Built-in, under-bed drawers will convert unused space into storage. In children's rooms, bunk beds are often the answer when a room must serve two or more occupants.

Throughout your house let general guidelines and common sense direct you in arranging furniture. Remember that although color and fabric make a room beautiful, it is the arrangement of furniture that determines whether or not it is livable. And every room must be livable as well as "lookable."

To Make Small Rooms Look Larger

In rooms where space is limited, the art of creating the feeling of space can be an important one. This can be accomplished through the adroit use of the principles and elements of design. First of all, put color and fabric to work for you, then look to the furniture. If you are selecting furniture, choose the following: small-scaled furniture (avoiding a doll-house effect); high shallow pieces for storage and display; tables with rounded corners, or with clear glass or plastic tops; chairs without arms or with see-through backs, or chairs made of clear plastic; upholstered pieces without skirts; and case pieces on legs rather than flush to the floor.

To make a small room appear larger.

Arrange furniture to make the most of every square foot of space. Align furniture against the wall, leaving the center of the room free. Hang shelves and high storage units from the ceiling and stop approximately a foot from the floor, allowing the perimeter of the room to be seen, thus adding to the feeling of space. Smaller units, such as serving tables, consoles, buffets, and desks may be hung to the wall, thereby eliminating the need for legs.

Lighting can do wonders in expanding space. Throw light on the ceiling or on the upper part of a wall or drapery to direct the eye upward. Use accessories to advantage. For example, let a mirror double the space or open out a corner. Use a few large accessories, not a hodgepodge of small objects. Your studied efforts will be well repaid, and the feeling of space you achieve may amaze you.

13
When a House Is a Home

If a house is a home, it will radiate personality. Not the personality of a decorator who has just put the last bibelot on the coffee table, but the personality of the people who live there. And because each household member is different and yet fits into the group, each room should have its unique characteristic within the over-riding theme of the home.

There is no such thing as instant decorating. The actual process may be done in a short time, but if successful it will be the result of long and careful planning. Nor does one often decorate an entire house at one time. But having the finished product in mind is important in helping to produce a feeling of unity.

The aim in redecorating should be to correct errors, give rooms a new freshness, perhaps a new mood. But don't discard old furniture indiscriminately; if it is a good design, refinish or recover it, but keep it to maintain the familiar look of home.

As families increase and children grow up, needs change, and often rooms take on different functions. In the Victorian house, the parlor was off bounds to children except on special occasions. The biggest room in the house was the well-equipped dining room, where the entire family gathered three times a day. Today we are lucky to get everyone together for one meal a day. Although the dining room is back, it is put to other uses as well as for eating.

In the early decades of this century, family meals and activities were carried on in one large open area. Togetherness was the thing. But carried to the extreme, togetherness can put a strain on personal relationships. Fortunately, *rooms* are back. The living room is off bounds to some activities, but it can be comfortably shared by all. In today's home, the family room is most often the center of activities. The high cost of floor space requires that bedrooms be small, but one does not need a large area for privacy and sleeping. All rooms, if well planned, can serve double duty when necessary.

The approach to a face-lifting or redecorating job will vary with each family and each house. Usually, the most urgent need is handled first. Assuming there is no particular urgency, a good place to begin is at the front door, not the inside, but the outside.

What a Difference a Door Makes

The front door more than any other architectural feature is what gives individuality to your house. It is the focus that calls attention to itself. Does your door "feel" right for your house? There are well-designed stock doors available for almost every style of architecture. Just be sure your door is suitable and well designed. The lover of traditional will probably sacrifice elsewhere to have a front door of which to be proud. Always avoid the elaborated pressed synthetic variety which smacks of pretense and fools no one.

If you wish to change the appearance of the front of your house, or just conceal your door from passersby, there are many ways of accomplishing this, and a small addition can produce a big change. Just a fence with clinging vines can supply an attractive barrier. A lattice fence will afford partial privacy, and with a change of walk and some potted plants, your entrance will take on a completely new look.

A simple lattice and vine afford beauty and privacy.

The Entrance Way

All homemakers will agree that an entrance hall is essential to the efficient working of a house. Basically, the foyer or entrance hall is a buffer between the outside and the inside living quarters. Its principal function is to serve as an efficient passageway directing traffic throughout the house and providing privacy to individual rooms.

Too often, the entry is dreary, and this is the last place this should happen. To anyone who steps inside the front door, the entry is a revealing glimpse of your home. Give it a definite feeling of cordial hospitality, even a touch of drama. Whatever the general theme of your home, play it up here. Since people do not linger in this area, you may be a bit bold with color and pattern so the initial impact may be an exciting one. Here is an excellent place to use one of the beautiful wallpapers available today. If the entrance is narrow, push out the walls by the use of a mural with a three-dimensional effect that leads the eye into a distant scene. When decorative paper is used, it is advisable to use a dado to take the wear off the lower part of the wall.

When you select the floor covering, keep in mind that the entrance is a passageway and must take traffic. One of the hard-surface materials such as brick, stone, terrazzo, travertine, or quartzite will provide a lifetime floor and will be easy to maintain. Or use a vinyl that simulates any of these. A well-anchored area or throw rug can add warmth and serve as a color transition into adjoining rooms.

A wall console takes no floor space. Mirror expands space.

Furniture should be kept to a minimum and placed against the wall. You need a small table to hold your purse or a package, a chair or bench for the paper boy, or for a seat while you're putting on your boots, and a mirror to take that last look, or to serve guests.

Lighting here need not be strong, but it should be strong enough that entering guests may see and be seen. Try some dramatic lighting. The result may be just the effect you are looking for.

When you have redecorated your entry and have given it a warm, intimate feeling, it will suggest to those who enter that your entire house has the same charming, hospitable atmosphere.

The Living Room

First of all, there should be a pleasant transition from the entry to the living room. Colors introduced in the entry should be carried into the adjoining room, not in the same items or the same proportions, but as a connecting link. For example, a color from the wallpaper in the entry may be used in the drapery or upholstery fabric in the living room.

If entry walls are papered with a pattern, it is advisable to keep the walls of the living room plain, either painted or paneled.

Your living room is shared by more people than any other room in your house; and because the general atmosphere should be relaxing, the color scheme should not be overpowering. Walls, floors, and fabrics should be carefully cooordinated, and an unmistakable aura of comfort should prevail. Don't hesitate to draw a furry rug over an area of carpet if it pleases you, and have an afghan handy for anyone who wishes to curl up.

Lighting can contribute much to the feeling of comfort. General lighting here should be soft and supplemented by special area lighting. Avoid an excess of indirect overhead lighting that has a tendency toward a commercial look. Well-chosen lamps, correctly located, will add to the feeling of comfort and charm.

When people are asked to describe a room they are particularly attracted to, they use the word *warmth* more than any other. But, it is a warmth that has nothing to do with temperature. Such things as color, fabrics, and wood add warmth; but more important than these are the little personal things that are so revealing: light that throws a pleasant glow, leafy plants, a bouquet of live flowers that speak of caring and add a human dimension, and books. Books on shelves and books that are lying about obviously being read give the feeling that someone will be coming in momentarily.

Next to the roof over your head, the most comforting feature you can have in your living room is a glowing fire on a cloudy day. What is there to compete with the good living one has with family and friends around the domestic hearth?

As the center of interest, the fireplace can set the decorating theme of the room. Today fireplaces take many shapes, from the free-standing stove to an open recess in a wall, framed with a variety of mantel facings. Old brick or rough stone are appropriate for rooms with a country or rustic look. Wood for facing is the most versatile and can be made to fit the decor of any room. The wood mantel and frame should harmonize with other woodwork in the room. You can get reproductions of all the traditional styles, as well as a great variety of styles for the contemporary setting. Marble facing is appropriate for a formal room, but many of the hard surface materials used for floors can be used successfully for fireplace facings in less formal settings. Fireplace tools and fittings are important accessories and should be chosen with care to be in keeping with the fireplace. If your fireplace is of a vintage not right for your room, or is poorly designed, a face-lift here would greatly enhance your decor. If you haven't a fireplace now, it should be high on your priority list for future remodeling.

A fireplace can set the decorating theme of the room.

In this room the spirit of the East is combined with contemporary. The high-backed chairs add dignity. The stacked cabinet and display case create compact storage. The uncluttered look allows changes for any and all occasions. *Courtesy of Hickory Manufacturing Co.*

In this open-kitchen/family room, the country look is achieved with warm quarry-tile floor that blends handsomely with the natural woods of the cabinets, chairs, and table and the rug and sofa of the adjoining area. The hanging basketry, copper kettles, and carriage lamp add further to the informality. *Courtesy of American Olean Tile Co.*

When guests enter your living room, what do you want them to see, a room that looks like a picture out of a magazine? Do you want them to be impressed by a look of affluence? Or do you want them to see a room that reflects you and your family—a room whose compelling warmth is an irresistible invitation to linger? Surely the latter should be your goal.

Dining Room

"As you eat, so will your guests love and remember you" is an old Roman saying. We could with reasonable certainty, add that "As you eat at home, so will your children remember."

The dining room was threatened with extinction during the decades following World War II—when open planning was the vogue, and the common practice was eating on a tray in front of the television, or from a bar in the kitchen. Now, however, the dining room is back and once again recognized as an important room, possibly *the* most important room.

There is no better time or place for children to learn the fundamentals of gracious behavior than at the dinner table, under the discipline of regular meals, where good manners and courtesy can be practiced in an appropriate setting. Around the dinner table is the best place for families to really learn about each other. At no other time or place can the art of conversation be fostered so naturally and successfully as around the dining room table, where every member is encouraged to participate, expressing his or her opinions and listening to the opinions of others. The dining room need not be formal, but privacy from the front door and the clutter of the kitchen is highly desirable. When you are planning your dining room, keep in mind that it should be pleasant, but that colors should not be obtrusive, because they may restrict the use of a variety of table settings for parties and seasonal holidays. The dining room is an ideal place for a mural wallpaper. A dado will protect the wall from chair bumps and finger marks.

Be sure the floor covering is practical. There is a hard-surface material to fit any decor. These coverings can be very handsome, and their maintenance is minimal. If you prefer carpet, choose one that is flat and easy to care for. A patterned one with all the food colors will conceal spots when the inevitable spills occur; a quick wipe-up will leave it none the worse. By all means avoid using a shag! It is wise, though, to keep the dining room in the same basic theme as the living room. Choose furniture suitably scaled to the room. The popular pedestal-base table gives maximum knee room, and the round and oval-shaped tables take up less room and make it easier to squeeze in an extra guest. To encourage friends to linger for long and stimulating conversation, choose chairs that are comfortable. Two-arm chairs, or host chairs, will add dignity and will serve as occasional chairs in the living room. If your dining room is large, a breakfront with shelves for china and glass and drawers for linens and silver is a handsome addition. If space is limited, a shallow chest or a wall-hung shelf for serving will suffice.

Lighting can do wonderful things for a dining room. Diffused light is easy on the eyes, and a well-chosen chandelier hung at a convenient height above the table will add charm and make silver and glass sparkle. Wall sconces can provide pleasant lighting, and candlelight, always flattering, will add a touch of glamor to the plainest table.

With space at such a premium, plan the dining room to serve several functions. Provide adjustable lighting for eating, studying, and table games. Your personal needs will determine the uses this room may serve.

The benefits derived from a separate dining room can have far-reaching results that will more than compensate you for your efforts and expense in providing this important part of your home.

The Kitchen

The kitchen, that pivotal room in the house that for so many years was neglected, has gone through many phases, each of which enjoyed some acceptance until in recent years. Now what has happened in the kitchen is nothing short of explosive. The overwhelming developments of modern technology have so deluged the modern homemaker with miracle materials, appliances, and gadgets that he or she is ready to seek refuge in the warmth and security of grandmother's old-fashioned kitchen. But, now you can enjoy the best of both worlds.

The many products available for use in today's complex kitchen require an efficient arrangement of working centers to satisfy the ideas and needs of the individual occupant. Most kitchens today have well-defined work centers for preparing, cooking, and refrigerating food, and they boast the necessary major appliances. But beyond this, what do you want *your* kitchen to be? Do you want a sociable kitchen? Do you enjoy conversation going on while you work behind the counter, or do you prefer to prepare meals uninterrupted in a more private, compact kitchen with every labor-saving device near at hand? Plan your kitchen to meet your personal desires.

Inherent in the kitchen design should be function and convenience. But what functions for one chef may not function for another. If you do a lot of baking, your baking center is of major importance. If you like your cooking utensils hanging overhead, or hidden away when not in use, plan your space accordingly.

To the joy of every homemaker, the pantry is back—and the bigger the better. There is nothing to equal it for convenient storage of food, large items, and an extra refrigerator.

Whatever the style of kitchen you choose, think of the durability and cleanability of all the materials. Today's market is fairly bursting with new plastic materials for floors, walls, counter tops, window sills, and furniture coverings, as well as handsome molded-plastic furniture. Walls should be easy to clean and maintain and should be resistant to wear and abuse. Decorative plywood with a tough plastic finish, wood paneling, scrubbable vinyl, impregnated paper, and paint are all practical.

Plan your lighting carefully. If you are building or remodeling, consider an illuminated ceiling and illuminated panels over counters. Good lighting here is a must.

No matter what the decor, utilize the most modern conveniences—but only up to a point. Somehow, word reaches every appliance store in your area if you are building or remodeling, and you will be bombarded by dealers who want to fill your kitchen with new appliances. It never seems to occur to them that you might intend to use the ones you have. If you are wise, you *will* use your old ones. Most new ones will not work as well. If the color you have is not right for your new scheme, there are miracle paints to do the job. Another word of caution: with all the gadgets being thrust upon us via television, beware! If we aren't selective, our kitchens will be cluttered with so-called labor-saving items, many of which only add extra work and take up valuable space.

Your kitchen ought to be the most pleasant room in the house. Whenever possible, have an east exposure that permits morning sunlight. For many people, the early morning hours are pretty bleak. But, who can feel depressed when you walk into a bright, cheery kitchen and see the morning sun streaming through airy sheers or colored chintz curtains and putting a sparkle on your budding plants? It gets the day off to a good start.

The Family Room

The family room came into being in the fifties. It takes on many forms, depending upon the individual family, but the objective usually is to provide flexible space for a wide variety of activities. The atmosphere most desired is one of hearth-centered congeniality, planned for easy upkeep. The heat circulating fireplace is a wise investment here. It can heat your room and save on energy and reduce utility bills.

For the ceiling, an acoustic tile is a good choice to muffle noise. For walls, woodlike vinyl paneling is attractive and takes hard knocks with little evidence. Scrubbable vinyl-coated wall covering is practical and is available in a wide range of textures and patterns. For durability, flexibility, and easy maintenance, a hard-surface flooring, or a vinyl simulating any of these is desirable. Area rugs are usually preferred by most active people, because the rugs can be moved easily.

Colors should be cheerful and fabrics should be strong, stain-resistant, and easily cleaned. Vinyl upholstering is excellent and comes in a wide range of colors, textures, and patterns. Furniture should be sturdy but easily movable for rearranging at a moment's notice. Pieces of furniture that can serve a dual role are particularly serviceable here. A sofa may serve as a bed for an overnight guest. Low tables may double as stools when covered with bright cushions. Tables that raise and lower may serve for coffee tables, games, and eating. A sofa-backed table becomes a buffet, and small stacking tables and stools can serve a number of uses. And of all the rooms in the house, probably the family room needs the most well-planned storage to take care of all the things that will be used here—such things as card tables, folding chairs, games, records, books, a movie screen, and a projector.

Ample overhead light is necessary here, as is lighting for specific areas. Track lights can bring dark corners into use, and installing them takes no particular skill.

The most preferred location for the family room is adjoining the kitchen. Young children can play within close range, and family activities can be a part of meal preparation. Wherever you locate your family room, make every effort to have it away from the bedroom wing. It should have easy access to the outside and the kitchen, and it should be planned to adjust as your needs change.

The Recreation Center

With the high and increasing cost of transportation and the inflated costs of movies and eating out, people are turning more and more to home for entertainment. Why not cash in on the trend and help to revive the pleasant pastime of sharing fun at home? Have a recreation center of your own. For most families, having both a family room and a recreation center is not possible. But sometimes the recreation center may be the more preferable of the two. Where to put it? Look around you. There may be space you didn't realize you had. Look in the attic. Perhaps wasted space there can be put to good use. Check the basement; it may have possibilities, and noise is muffled in a downstairs location. What about turning the garage into a recreation center and extending the roof for a carport? There may even be a room already finished that can be taken over after some not-too-serious shifting.

When once the space is decided upon, start planning from the floor upward. Traffic and wear will be heavy, so select a good tile, quality vinyl, or heavy-duty nylon carpet. A carpet that can be rolled up for dancing will be practical. You may wish to choose one of the new fun carpets that are gaily printed with gameboards such as hopscotch, tic-tac-toe, chess, checkers, and others. Vinyl-laminated paneling is a good choice for walls.

Furniture must be sturdy and easily movable. To promote social interaction with lots of good talk, lounge chairs and sofas must be comfortable. Consider covering them with carpet for long wear. For some furniture, use vinyl. It is soft, wears well, and comes in a wide range of colors and textures.

Listening to records and tapes will be a major pastime. Place the speakers where they provide the best sound. Television watching is inevitable, so provide for it.

Tables are necessary. To avoid breakage and scratches, select sturdy vinyl-topped ones to be used for games such as chess, checkers, gin rummy, backgammon, and bridge. A billiard table will encourage competitive activity and help develop coordination.

Left*: This handsome master bedroom with its warm walls, natural woods, and sturdy canopy bed is enhanced by the rug with its earth colors and natural design and by the handcrafted bedspread and the soft leather chair. The cloistered look provides comfort and relaxation. *Courtesy of Drexel Heritage Furnishings.

Encourage a sing-along by including an upright piano. You may even find an old player piano at a reasonable price. It will give hours of pleasure. A fireplace with a wide hearth for roasting weiners and marshmallows and for just relaxing will add a warm, friendly atmosphere. Keep the fire burning on cloudy days.

A pull-down screen to show home movies and slides can be permanently installed at little cost. You will need extra folding chairs. The canvas director chairs are inexpensive and can be colorful, and they are easily brought out of storage to handle a crowd. Homemade bean bags and large floor cushions invite informality and relaxation.

A soda bar is always a popular spot. You may even want to create an old-fashioned ice cream parlor theme. Eating is such a social thing that wherever goodies are available, people will gather.

Recreation centers can be planned to encourage not only activities with family members alone but also involvement with school, church, and community affairs. A room that is always open and ready for a committee meeting or a rehearsal will surely become a focal point for gatherings of all ages. What better use could be made of space? Anything that makes young people *want* to be home is worth a lot of planning and effort—and even sacrifice.

The Master Bedroom

Decorating your own bedroom is different from decorating any other room in your house. Your bedroom is private and personal, and there you may close the door without apology. Here you don't have to be concerned about traffic and wear and tear. Your main consideration should be twenty-four-hour comfort and convenience. Comfort does not require a large room, but it does require the best mattress you can get, a curl-up chair or two, and well-organized space.

From the outset, keep in mind that the master bedroom is a room shared by a man and a woman. Select colors that you both enjoy; chances are they will be warm, earthy tones. Coordinate your colors with distinction and taste to set the proper mood.

The luxurious element in your room is the fabric. It adds softness, color, and elegance. But avoid a bedspread that is too delicate. You deserve one you can lie on without feeling guilty. The market abounds in sumptuous-looking bedspreads that satisfy this requirement and can take normal use without wrinkling or soiling easily. Provide draw drapery or window blinds to keep morning light out when necessary.

Before actual decorating begins, decide what purposes the room will serve, other than repose. A bedroom and a study can be a very happy combination. Shelves of books, a big desk, a swivel chair, and good lighting will create a treasured haven.

The master bedroom needs two comfortable chairs that "fit" the occupants, and at least one should be a comfortable curl-up variety. Bedside tables are necessary and should have shelves and surfaces that will withstand moisture. They should also be large enough to hold a book, a glass, and a telephone.

The currently popular king-sized bed becomes more predominant as a focal point of the room and as such demands special attention in your planning. If you have always longed for a canopy bed, you may have it. A sturdy four-poster can give the room a quiet dignity. And don't overlook a few personal luxuries that can add much to your feeling of well being, such as a warm throw for cool-weather snuggling, attractive sheets and blankets, and comfortable backrests for reading.

Adequate light, conveniently placed, will add immeasurably to your comfort. Provide a night-time dimmer for safety. If reading in bed is your pleasure, provide sufficient light for it. The hang-down variety gives excellent illumination and takes no space. Personal choice and the way you live should be your guides to furnishing your most personal room.

The Child's Room

We may never know how much the houses we live in contribute to the complete growth of children, but we know that a well-planned physical environment can help guide their emotional development. If the child is provided a private retreat, no matter how small, it will contribute to his feeling of self-esteem and well-being and will be the best gift you can give him. A child's room is a private world and should be respected as such by other members of the family. It is a place to have pets and friends; a place to store things, display things, and hide things. It is a place to read, to work at hobbies, to munch, and to dream.

A child's bed is not just for sleeping—it is a springboard, a hideaway, and a stage; so plan for it. Use heavy stain-resistant canvas for a fitted bed cover, and fashion a canopy or a tent for hours of make-believe.

A child's room is used for much more than sleeping. Here, homemade plywood boxes are stacked by and under the window to hold toys and books. Topped with cushions, boxes become a window seat. Others become tables. A sprightly wallpaper, colorful blinds, and soil-resistant fabric complete a room in which to have friends for hours of play. *Courtesy of Imperial Wallcoverings and Tennessee Tufting.*

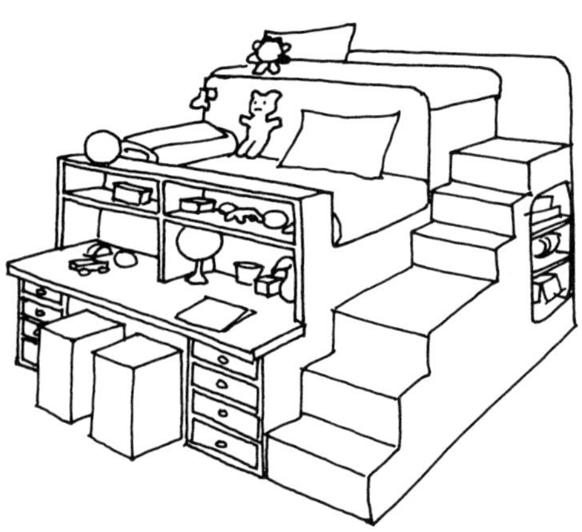

Build a bed on a mound. Use the mound for storage and a work area.

Try building two bunk beds atop a storage platform. It is a good way to use space, and it will delight girls and boys.

Since children's toys inevitably get pushed under the bed, why not use that space for pull-out drawers? Equip closets with rods hung at reachable height. They can easily be raised as years add inches to children.

A fantasy wall mural can be fun. Try painting one yourself with your child's help. A big magnetic or cork bulletin board to provide space for children's displays is a must. Be sure to have a simple desk equipped with adequate light. A do-it-yourself one will do very well. This will encourage good study habits.

The room should be decorated with the child's help so that it will express his or her personality. The smallest space, if skillfully planned, can serve two children,

Children grow up. A young lady may choose to flood her room with a delicate print. An eyelet-topped table, chairs for long talks with friends, and mounds of colorful cushions for snuggling—a small room becomes a teenager's delight. *Courtesy of Imperial Wallcoverings and Collins and Aikman.*

with some privacy for each. And with wise long-range planning and frequent modifications, a bedroom can serve from toddler to teen.

A Room for a Girl

The girl's room is a private affair, and from an early age she should have a voice in how it is decorated. If she loves—and feels at ease in—a feminine atmosphere, there are wallpapers, fabrics, floor coverings, and furniture to delight her. If she prefers dark walls and floors, and fabrics with dogs and horses, these too are available, and she should surround herself with them.

As she grows older, a girl's interests may change, and her room should reflect this change. Current magazines provide up-to-date previews of the newest

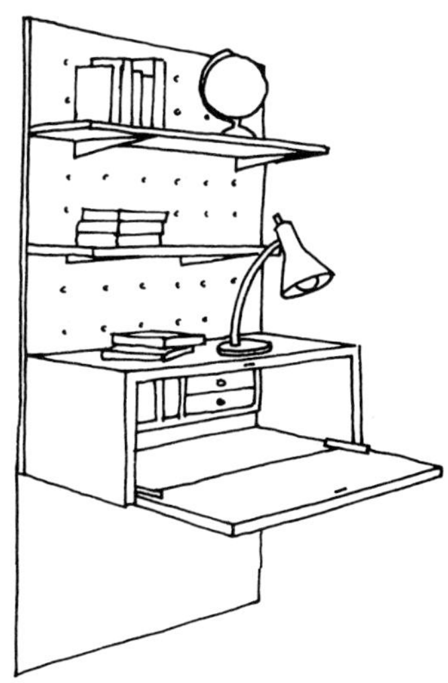

A pegboard and a box with a hinged door combine to create an inexpensive desk.

Two dividers create a study area and two beds with privacy.

colors, fabrics, and furniture—with new ideas for their use. An awareness of current trends, as well as a knowledge of traditional and contemporary styles, will enable a young lady to choose what appeals to her in creating a private environment that will reflect her own personality, an environment in which she can function at her optimum level.

A Room for a Boy

As the boy changes, so should his room. Don't embarrass a preteen boy by keeping his room like a nursery. Individual needs must always determine what changes should be made, and when, but from year to year the maturing child requires some altering of his physical environment. Let the boy have a voice in decorating his room. If his choices are not yours, this is unimportant. The important thing is that the room expresses *his* personality. He will take greater pride in it if he feels it is his.

Almost any room that serves many needs should have a generous-sized bulletin board. A boy may want one covering a complete wall, where he can put all manner of pinups for his ever-changing enthusiasms. It will be a handy place to exhibit his schoolwork and may stimulate creativity. Whatever his interests, they will be reflected in the things he displays. Take this as a clue to areas in which to offer encouragement and guidance. A boy's room is his private kingdom. Respect it as such, and he will respect your room. If you find that your teenage boy spends many quiet hours in his room behind closed doors, that he frequently has friends there, that the room gets messy and dirty, and that an occasional thing gets broken, there is no cause for alarm. The room is serving its intended purposes.

The Bathroom

Once a purely functional room at the end of the hall, today's bathroom has become the glamor room of the American home. Today, function and luxury are combined, and the room once hidden behind closed doors is frequently exposed to sky, garden, terrace, and in some instances, to other rooms of the house (with screens or sliding glass doors for privacy). What was once a small, sterile room has become a powder room, a dressing room, and even a sitting room with stained-glass windows, easy chairs, and a couch for lounging and massage.

The fixtures for the bathroom have kept abreast of the trend. Recalling the splendor of Rome, tubs may be sunken and deep enough for standing. They may be in the center of the room, in all shapes and sizes, and with built-in seats. Beautiful new basins are made of marble, onyx, hand-carved shells, or china. Manufacturers have coordinated all important accessories such as shower curtains, towel bars, and soap dishes.

For the average home owner, most of these things are undoubtedly extreme and probably out of reach, but with the wonderful new materials available, you can update your present bathroom, giving it a feeling of glamor, without too much expense. When you build or remodel your bathroom, keep in mind the kind of use it will receive and plan your decorating accordingly. For the family bathroom, easy upkeep should have top priority. Today this does not present a problem, with a market bursting with scurubbable vinyls for every purpose in all colors and patterns. Carpet is not a sensible choice for a bathroom that has heavy use.

A bathroom must have ample storage for such items as towels, cosmetics, and soiled clothes, and good lighting is essential. Mirrors for makeup and grooming are a must, and the effect they can create by doubling light and expanding space is a bonus.

In recent years, the bathroom in America has become a fetish, and the number of bathrooms now in a house has taken precedence over the design or arrangement of space. If houses are going to be provided in a price range that most people can afford, the bathroom will have to return to the functional room it once was, and with one or two to a family. It could be done, and people would survive—maybe rather well.

Decorating—An Ongoing Process

Not often do people redecorate an entire house at one time. So, if you aren't able to, don't be unhappy.

A bathroom need not cost a lot of money. Vinyl wall covering, removable carpet with small rug protectors, louvered blinds, color-coordinated towels, and plants here create a look of sophistication. And you can do it yourself. *Courtesy of Imperial Wallcoverings and Tennessee Tufting.*

This bathroom is the result of careful planning and some hard work. A do-it-yourselfer cabinet, vinyl paper, shuttered window, and removable carpet complete just the right background for ornate wicker and living plants. *Courtesy of Imperial Wallcoverings and Tennessee Tufting.*

Keep in mind that decorating is "doing" and is an ongoing process. Remind yourself of the "charm of the incomplete." Besides, there is pleasure in anticipation, and by doing one room or getting one new thing at a time, your decisions will more likely be right than if it were possible to do everything at one time.

Few of us can afford to have all the new things we think we need in our homes, and this is good. Use what you have. If a piece of wood furniture was good when you got it, it is still good. You may want to shift some things from one room to another, and put them to a different use. Try it. You may even find yourself returning to a prominent spot in your living room the very first piece of furniture you ever bought.

Always keep your over-all plan in mind, and have a nest-egg set aside for an important down payment. At the most unexpected time you may see exactly the thing you have been looking for. If you do—get it!

Don't feel sorry for yourself because you have to count your pennies. The necessity of getting the most we can for each decorating dollar makes us more prudent in our purchases and the end result is usually better because of it.

Be an Informed Consumer

To save money and, at the same time, get the things you need for your home, be an informed consumer.

- Read good current magazines regularly. They frequently feature in-depth articles on what to look for when purchasing items for your home.
- Check your daily newspapers. They carry articles that are informative and often include helpful buying tips. Make it a habit to look for them.

- Inquire regularly about literature published by manufacturers of all household articles from hard-floor surfacing to how-to-make your own drapery. Many magazines carry ad coupons that you need only clip and mail for valuable and dependable information.
- Watch for model home shows, but go with a critical eye and an inquiring mind. The new products you will see may be of help to you, and literature is usually available. But do not accept all you see as "good." Unfortunately, too many such homes are badly designed and poorly decorated. Too often these houses are used as brash pushers for household products; rarely will they provide answers to the problems you are living with.
- Write to the Superintendent of Documents, U.S. Printing Office, Washington, D.C., and ask to be put on the mailing list for monthly pamphlets that contain the latest information on household appliances.
- Contact the home economics agent in your county. He or she will have up-to-date materials on almost anything for the home, and they are often free for the asking.
- Use the library nearest you. And browse in bookstores. If you get one useful idea, it will more than make up for the price of the book.
- One of the best sources of help is your local hardware and building supply store. Many of these stores have become total home centers staffed with knowledgeable personnel qualified to assist you in planning home projects, as well as in selection of materials and equipment. They also will likely have a library of consumer literature on every subject, from selecting your drapery tiebacks to installing a dishwasher.

New items are entering the market almost daily. Many become life-long products; others fall by the wayside. So beware! Don't be a guinea pig. Be sure that your purchase has been sufficiently tested.

A house can be built in a few months, but a home is never really finished. Creating a home requires a lot of hard work, dedication, and constant adjusting and refining. But most of all a home takes a lot of love and a lot of living.

14
Little Things--The Most Revealing

Don't overlook the importance of little things. These are the accessories that put the finishing touch and the stamp of your personality to your rooms. More than any other element of furnishing, they reflect your taste and your individuality. They can be almost anything, but they should never be just something to fill up space. If an item is neither useful, beautiful, nor meaningful to you, it has no place in your home. It is much better to leave the space empty until you find something that answers at least one of these requirements. Some accessories have a necessary function, such as clocks, lamps, mirrors, fire tools, and cushions, but these also should enhance the room and must be chosen with discrimination. Small articles of household furniture that come under the classification of accessories, such as wastebaskets and umbrella stands, are necessary and functional. If they are not beautiful, they should not be conspicuous. Accessories need not be new. An old family heirloom can add distinctive charm and character to an otherwise dull room. Objects that may have been collecting dust in attics for years may be salvaged by an ingenious homemaker.

The desire to display one's prized possessions is universal. If the items you have collected are worth acquiring, they are worth displaying. Things gathered from here and there on family trips and outings, or items passed down from earlier generations can create a common family bond. We find a sense of pleasure and a certain security in seeing the same things from day to day, and your personal collections will imbue your home with something which no decorator can provide—the unmistakable stamp of your personal taste. But you must know when to stop! A display of too many things, too many pictures, too many souvenirs, and too many wedding presents can become a hodgepodge.

Door knockers

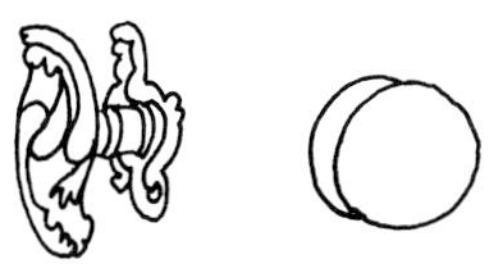

Door knobs

Drawer pulls

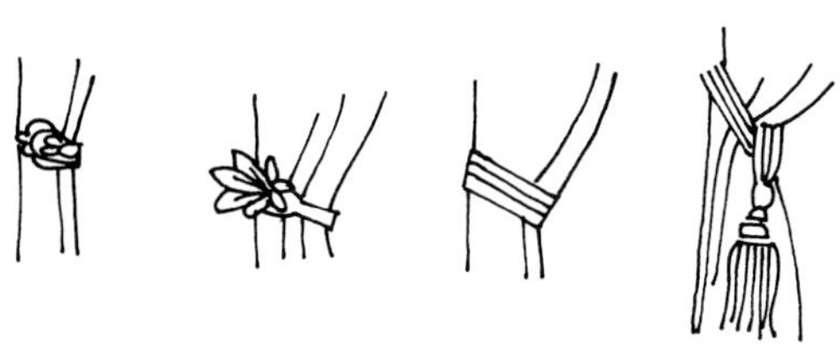

Tiebacks

Little things make the difference.

One of the greatest challenges in decorating your home is making beautiful compositions out of the little things you handle every day. The secret lies in training your eye to see beauty, form, and space relationships. When arranging a number of items, you can avoid a cluttered look by using items which are in some way related, such as in shape, color, or purpose. Some small items that are used frequently can be arranged on a tray for convenience and a feeling of unity. This will prevent a messy look.

Displaying Art

The art we choose to live with and display, probably the most personal thing of all in our homes, tells more about us than any other single thing. Don't despair if you cannot afford an original oil or watercolor by your favorite artist. There are numerous alternatives, many of which, if chosen with discrimination, may prove satisfactory. There are excellent prints on the market, both traditional and modern, for very little money, and a good print is better than a mediocre original. If you love contemporary art, there is an enormous range from which to choose. There may be an amateur artist near you. Have confidence in your own taste; if you like the paintings, don't be afraid to use them. The price very likely will be within your reach.

A picture can be enhanced or detroyed by the way it is framed. To achieve the most pleasing result possible is more complex than one might suspect, but with a little study and observation it can be accomplished. Some pictures do not call for a frame; they look complete without it. When a frame is used, it should never dominate the picture but should be chosen only if it is appropriate for the subject and the style of rendering. Frames can repeat wood tones of furniture or can be painted or gilded. A traditional oil demands a rich, heavy frame and should be framed without glass or mat. Pencil sketches, etchings, and watercolors are more delicate and should be simply framed and, usually, matted. Modern paintings are usually best with narrow moldings of wood, brass, or chrome.

The items that can be hung on walls to give character to a room are innumerable and are determined only by personal taste. Use your imagination and your creative urge. Make a handsome collage. Press and mount flowers and leaves, framing them identically and hanging them in a group. Make a lighted shadow box from an old picture frame, line it with fabric, and display small memorabilia. Group small pictures on a piece of plywood covered with velvet. Whatever you hang on your wall, let it frankly reflect your taste. And place it so that it looks as though it was meant for that very spot.

Mirrors

Distinctive in their inherent beauty, mirrors are a functional and decorative medium in today's home. They add beauty, increase the apparent spaciousness of a room, and are one of the decorator's most helpful tools. They can be found in almost any size and in frames to fit any decor. Watch for secondhand furniture with good mirrors that can be removed and used for any number of purposes. Mirror techniques offer easy and often inexpensive solutions to decorating problems. When rooms feel too enclosed, mirrors can multiply space. A full-wall mirror will double the appar-

A mirror in a corner can give an illusion of space and double the light supply.

A standing screen creates a foyer and a private writing area.

ent size of a room and open up a narrow hallway. The corner of a room may be pushed out by fitting a mirror into the corner and extending it from floor to ceiling. Through decorative know-how, mirrors may be used not only to add beauty and multiply space but distribute and double light, brighten dark areas and bring life into a room. Because of their myriad uses, mirrors have steadily increased in popularity through the years until today they play a virtually indispensable role in modern decorating.

Screens

One of the most graceful and economical means of individualizing your surroundings is by the use of a standing screen, and there is a wide variety on the market today. The versatile shutter type with movable louvers may be used anywhere. Wood frames containing light-filtering materials such as fiber glass, caning, pierced metal, or filigree in a wide assortment of designs from geometrics to exotic arabesques are familiar. With ingenuity and very little money you can fashion your own screen to suit your particular needs. The simplest frame with hinges attached will serve as a foundation for whatever decorative medium you choose. Covered with a handsome flocked or foiled paper, it will give a touch of glamor; a quaint geometric will add a rustic look. When covered with the right fabric, a screen can do wonders. It provides an excellent opportunity to "show off" creative ideas with such things as découpage, stitchery, colorful yarns, beads, shells, acorns, small pine cones, and bits of broken mirrors. Let your imagination run riot. Dare to be original. A decorative screen may give an architectural quality to a room, may set or enhance the room's decor, provide a backdrop for a furniture grouping in a room with limited wall space, substitute for side drapery, and serve as the room's focal point. In addition to its decorative values, a screen can serve many functional purposes. It is the number one multipurpose item in your home and can easily be moved from one room to another.

Lamps

The portable lamp can give a room decorative qualities that no other medium can provide. When a lamp is lighted, the eye is automatically drawn to it, so it should be chosen carefully as to scale and style. During the daytime, it should fit harmoniously into the room, thus becoming an asset to the decor at all times. Unfortunately, the market abounds with lamps, portable and hanging, that are nothing short of monstrosities. Avoid them like the plague. Your key to selecting lamps and lighting fixtures should be simplicity and suitability. Well-designed lamps in both modern and period styles *are* available. Apply your best sense of taste in selecting lamps, not only to avoid mediocrity, but to achieve personal distinction.

Books

"A room without books is a body without a soul," said Cicero. Books can do more than anything—except people—to add life and friendliness to a home. A room never needs to feel empty of furnishings if books are visible. With so many types of flexible shelves readily available and easily installed, books can be kept anywhere. A book wall can be constructed easily and in-

Make a divider.

expensively. Shelves can be fitted in niches, in odd corners, around doorways and windows, utilizing unused space most anywhere. No room has a mood that would preclude books. No color scheme is so complete that it cannot be enhanced by the warm tones and textures of books. The entrance hall is an excellent place for them. They require little space, create a warm friendly atmosphere, and are accessible to all areas of the house. Every child's room needs bookshelves at a height that the child can reach. In any bedroom headboards are convenient storage for your bedtime reading. Kitchens need handy shelves for reference books. The living room and family room should have ample bookshelves to hold the ever-expanding collection of books for the entire family. Books, like flowers, are never out of place; like friends, they should always be close at hand.

Plants

Are you a victim of the indoor gardening fever that began sweeping the country about a decade ago? Or do you find house plants more of a headache than a joy after having discovered warped furniture and mildewed rugs from drippings? You're right: water and drainage can present a problem. But don't let this keep you from using them. The solution is simple: equip your containers with adequate trays, and don't flood your plants. More plants are killed by drowning than by drought.

Of all the accessories that make up the final touches of your home, nothing can do for a room what live foliage or a bouquet of flowers can do. Just by its presence, a plant can add warmth and life to a room. That

Books Go Almost Anywhere

Under a stairway.

Around a doorway.

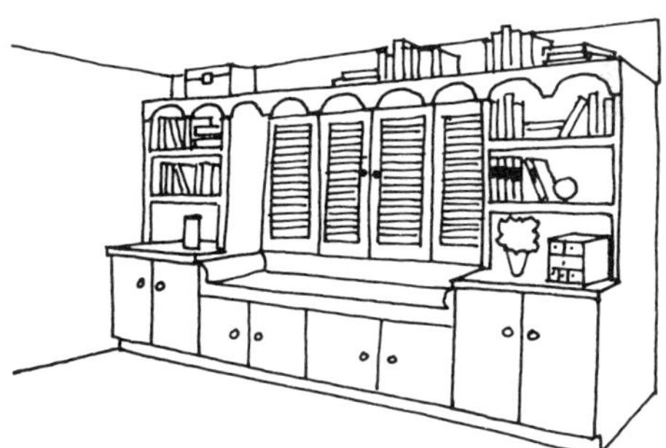

Around a window.

In a room divider or backdrop

Replace a window with a greenhouse.

Fill a kitchen window with herbs.

What could be prettier than a window full of plants hanging at varying heights? Folding screens are attached to the sides to be used if needed. *Courtesy of Imperial Wallcoverings and Collins and Aikman.*

you love your home and take pride in its beauty is evidenced by the extra effort that fresh plants and flowers require. Plants also can help solve some of your decorating problems. They can liven up a somber room, brighten your kitchen, serve as a room divider, and substitute for curtains or drapery to mention only a few of their many uses. Pots of plants blooming on the window sills, greenery hanging in the corners and trailing over the shelves, these can bring life into your room. But when is enough enough? You *can* overdo it! Who needs an indoor jungle where you can't get out of a chair without catching your head in the branches of a tree, and where moving about requires a machete?

Plants can be used throughout the house so long as they don't obstruct traffic. A corner window that is sometimes difficult to decorate is an excellent place for a plant grouping. Hang the plants at varying levels, and place them on blocks of different heights on the floor. They are out of the line of traffic, and louvered blinds can control the light. Because of the humidity, plants are happy in a bathroom, although they may need artificial light.

Do you enjoy cooking with herbs? If you do, make an herb garden in your kitchen window. Watching them grow is fun, and having fresh herbs near at hand when you need them is a real convenience.

Small plants make a better showing if grouped together, but sometimes a tiny plant tucked into an unexpected spot gives a touch of beauty and pleasure.

For those who get hooked on plants and can't get enough, a good solution is a home greenhouse. It may be free standing or attached to the house. There are any number of sizes and shapes. It can be do-it-yourself project, or your local contractor can construct it for you. Try making a greenhouse to replace a window. Plants sit on glass or metal mesh shelving. The aluminum greenhouse window comes fully assembled with complete installation instructions.

Wherever you put them, enjoy your plants. Don't let them become a burden. What, more than the feeling of perpetual springtime in your house, can keep away the glooms.

The little things that give the finishing touches to your room can enhance, detract, or overpower all other elements. So, stifle the temptation to overdo. If you

Who could feel depressed in a kitchen like this? An easy-to-maintain cobble-square vinyl floor, sleek bentwood chairs, a colorful print on the wall and table, and blooming plants in the windows add up to a room that would delight anyone. *Courtesy of Armstrong Cork Co.*

Against the natural-looking wall covering here, the sleek lines of the parson's table add just the right contrast. The flower containers and the tureen provide an important personal touch. The well-chosen chandelier and green plants complete the accessories in the small area. ***Courtesy of Imperial Wallcoverings and Collins and Aikman.***

feel that your room lacks character, search until you find just the right thing. Look for small accessories with subtle motifs that strengthen the theme of your room; or by contrast, add a touch of excitement. Never buy something just to fill up space. Leave room for that something very special you'll run onto one day. Whatever you use, it should be in keeping with the quality you have established in your home.

15
The Joys of Junking

Are you a junkyard addict? If you are, you know that the rewards of scavenging in a cobwebby junk shop are something that most people know nothing about. If you are one of those fortunate enough to discover beauty where others see only "junk," you know how gratifying it can be. The satisfaction of making something useful, even beautiful, out of what someone else has discarded not only saves money but satisfies a creative urge. The worthwhile items that can be salvaged by one with a trained eye are unlimited. If a piece of furniture is of good wood and solid construction and is well designed, it is worth refinishing. Many a prized antique has been rescued after being hidden for years under numerous layers of paint. To bring old furniture back to life does not require any special talent. What it does require is desire, patience, and hard work; but the feeling of accomplishment one feels in restoring a good piece of wood to its original beauty is worth the sore muscles and broken fingernails. Learn to upholster. This too is hard work, but it pays big dividends.

New Uses for Old Things

Furniture discarded because of its poor design can sometimes be restyled to serve a modern need. With a little imagination, this undertaking can be profitable and rewarding. Second-hand and good-will stores abound in such items. Never pass up a pile of "junk" without giving it a close scrutiny. Large pieces can often be taken apart and used for a variety of purposes. Old radio cabinets have many possibilities. Try placing an old-fashioned china cabinet on top of a radio cabinet. Line the china cabinet with velvet, install interior lighting, add new hardware to both, and you may have a charming and valuable focal point for your room.

An old filing cabinet may be turned into a kneehole desk. A long, outdated sewing machine base—when a

A long-outdated sewing-machine base with a plywood top laminated with vinyl or wood veneer becomes a handsome buffet with a Mediterranean look.

Old dressers that are too deep for today's limited space can be cut vertically and put side by side to form shelves.

Watch for unusual ideas. Two old hitching posts, bolted to the floors, make unique newel-posts.

plywood top laminated with vinyl or wood veneer is added—becomes a handsome buffet with a Mediterranean look. Brass beds need only to be polished and backed with colored felt or velvet, and a fashionable headboard results. Old iron gates make effective headboards. All manner of old beds can be restyled, cut down, painted, and padded.

Old dressers that are too deep for today's limited space can be cut vertically and put side by side to form shelves; cabinets that are too tall can be cut horizontally and placed side by side. A dresser becomes a chest of drawers when the mirror is removed and hung to expand space elsewhere; an outdated buffet becomes a chest when the legs are removed; a sturdy round table with legs lowered becomes a coffee table; cut in half, it makes a pair of consoles.

Many objects that have been collecting dust in attics for years may be salvaged and put to new uses by one with a perceptive eye and a generous imagination. One resourceful woman found a pair of old hitching posts with carved wooden horse heads that she used as unique newel posts in her ultramodern entrance way. A grandfather clock case, when refinished, can become a handsome nook for a telephone; a Victorian coat hanger will make a marvelous towel rack in a family bathroom; a baby's cradle, with rockers removed, inverted and topped with glass, makes a fitting coffee table; an old steamer trunk can become both a chest of drawers and a cabinet to hold a television (or paint it and put it on a stand, and it will serve double duty as a coffee table and as storage). A partial set of dining room chairs with ornately carved headrails and front legs have great possibilities: (1) two complete chair

Put an older steamer trunk to use.

The result of four chairs, some imagination, and work.

backs form an attractive headboard, (2) two top rails mounted on a backboard make a handsome cornice, (3) one chair seat and four front legs become a stool. Cover all three in the same fabric.

For decorative purposes, a metal register from an obsolete hot-air furnace can be the top for a lamp or coffee table; ornately carved table legs may form the base for a new, handsome, glss-top table; an odd piece of wood carving may show up as a decorative wall shelf or bracket; an old picture frame supported by a luggage rack will make a coffee table; old window frames or shutters placed against a windowless wall when filled with plants and lighted from behind will create the illusion of a garden room; metal rims from an auto junkyard, when fastened together with epoxy glue, painted and cushioned, will double as a low table and extra seating; and old window shutters can conceal unsightly radiators.

The things to be found and the purposes they can serve are endless; and the satisfaction of turning an eyesore into a useful or decorative object is a real incentive to keep searching. Availability of lucrative sources will vary in different areas but some can be found in most lucrative localities. Used furniture stores and good-will stores of various kinds are almost everywhere. Watch for new acquisitions by making regular visits. Articles of best value do not often remain long. Don't overlook items that have been languishing, sometimes for years, in basements and dark corners. This is where an occasional treasure is found. Check your local newspapers for items offered at real "sacrifice prices." Rummage through family attics and garage sales. Attend auctions and be on hand when old buildings in your area are being torn down. You never know when you may run onto a real treasure.

When Is a Bargain a Bargain?

Everyone loves a bargain, but the word *budget* for some people has a negative connotation. When referring to decorating, some people think budgeting means furnishing a home with something less than the best; to others it means buying cheap furnishings.

Budget buying should mean getting the most value for the money you spend. Getting your money's worth involves knowing value and recognizing that a bargain is not what you *pay,* but what you *get* for what you pay. It means being happy with what you purchased. Being sorry for what you bought is waste. To avoid

Old iron fencing turns into an authentic-looking Spanish headboard.

The result of junking. The back of the cupboard was missing! So make a feature out of a fault. The footboard was gone. It wasn't needed. The polished headboard is a beauty. A large wooden spool becomes a table. The baby buggy was retrieved from an attic. The only new item is the wicker chair. *Courtesy of United Wallcoverings and Collins and Aikman.*

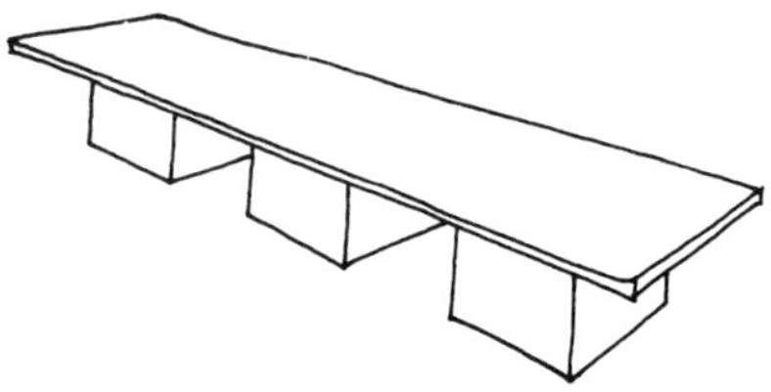

Three cubes and a board become a coffee table.

The Parson's table has many uses.

waste and mistakes in your purchases, be honest when you shop. Don't pretend you are going to get something you know you cannot afford. Decide in advance and frankly state what you can pay. Then search until you find good design that fits your needs and your pocketbook.

Know Your Resources

A real bargain seldom happens by chance. You must always be on the look out for value. Learn to be a shrewd shopper. Know the resources in your community. Besides knowing the best places to shop for home furnishings, are you familiar with the brick and lumber yards in your area? Bargains galore may be awaiting you there. By all means, check them regularly for rejects and scrap lumber. With imagination and a

By day a sofa.

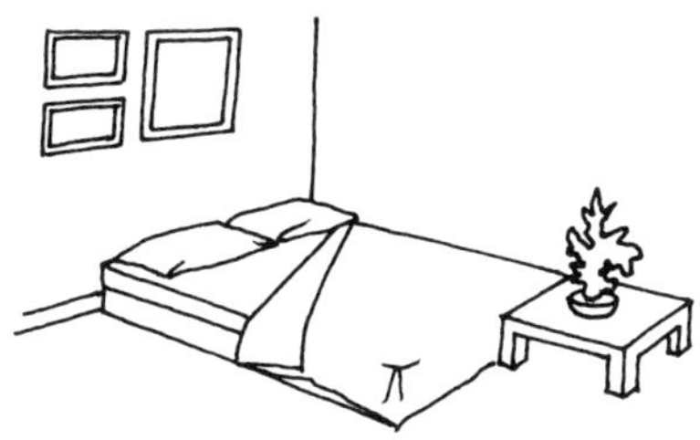

By night a bed.

little skill, these can be the "makings" of useful and necessary household items.

Odd lengths and scrap pieces of lumber obtained at little or no cost often can be utilized for do-it-yourself items. Squares of wood when made into cubes and topped by a stock door or plywood slab will make a long coffee table. The cubes also can be useful in children's rooms later on. Scrap pieces of wood supplemented by additional lumber can produce furniture items at surprisingly low cost and with pleasing results. The well-known Parsons table, which is a must for a room with a modern look and is at home in any room, is easy to make. A sturdy, easily constructed boxlike base, when fitted with a single mattress and back cushions, can become a sofa by day and a bed by night. The same type of base built higher will make an excellent coffee table, and both pieces will conceal all manner of storage items. The table may house a record player and records.

The Possibilities of Stock Wood Items

Wood molding can rejuvenate your home in many ways. For example, give a room a traditional atmosphere by applying moldings to plain walls to simulate paneling: add a chair rail to protect your walls against bumps; put a base molding on to protect walls against mops, brooms, and the vacuum cleaner; add moldings to kitchen cabinets, doors, and headboards for a custom look; or use them for picture frames, lamp bases, or wherever your creative urge dictates.

Turn a plain door into something special.

Beveled wood blocks have many uses. Glue them to drawers, to the sides of painted case furniture, or to a plain door to give the effect of carving. When blocks are added to the lower part of a wall below a chair rail, they produce the illusion of a wood-paneled dado.

Useful Articles from Odds 'n' Ends

Wood balusters—old or new—have many uses. Large ones mounted on wooden blocks with a screw or nail on the top become attractive candle holders. Rows of balusters glued to a frame will make a handsome divider. Many odd pieces of lumber can be converted into useful household items. Simple, wall-hung storage units are easy to make and are inexpensive. A fold-down desk or serving table is useful and takes little

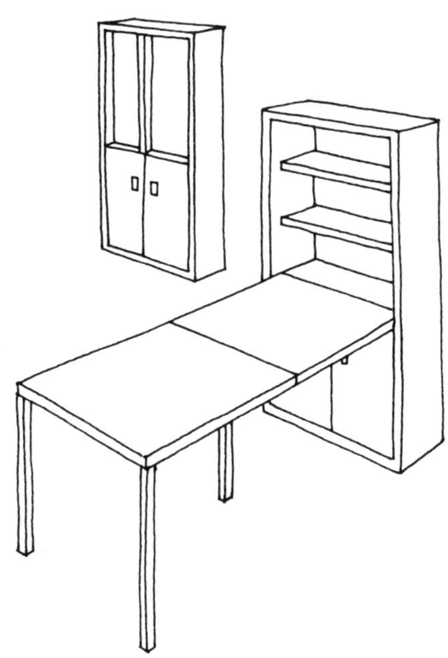

A dual-purpose cabinet takes little space—a great do-it-yourself item.

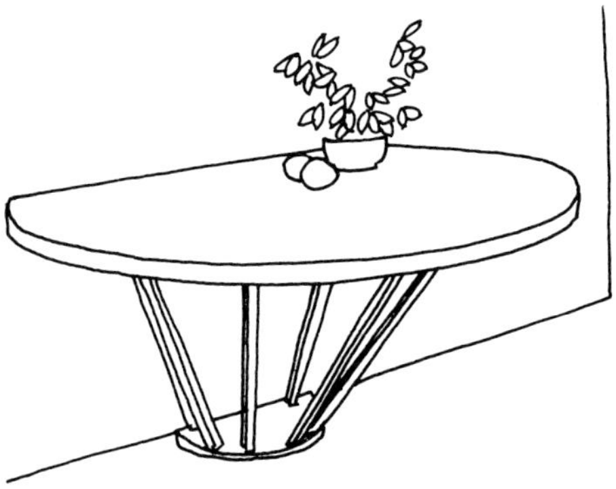

Conserve space with an inexpensive built-in table.

An abandoned capital with part of a column becomes a handsome table base.

material and little space. One half-circle of plywood with a laminated plastic top supported on a pedestal of angled wood strips makes an excellent table for a small area.

Keep your eyes open for discarded crating lumber. It can be put to many uses. When stained or sprayed, it takes on the appearance of barn wood that is so popular. Don't overlook the possibilities of orange packing boxes. They needn't be of a uniform size. When lined and edged with wallpaper or fabric, they may be stacked to provide colorful storage. Watch for discarded packing barrels. You need only fasten a round piece of plywood on the top and skirt it with a fabric, and you have a table for many purposes. Be on the lookout for wooden spools abandoned by utility companies. These make sturdy tables, come in many sizes, and are usually free.

The Word Gets Around

It won't be long until the word will get around that you are a lumberyard pack rat and a junkyard buff or both. This too may pay off. When people learn that you love old things to "fix up," odd pieces of dilapidated furniture may begin showing up on your doorstep. Be on your guard, though. After you have spent hours and days removing paint, gluing joints, and refinishing these orphaned items, the original owner may see the restored discard in your house and want it back. This happens! Don't let it bother you. Keep it, of course, and enjoy it.

Off the Highways and onto the Byways

Some of the greatest joys of junking are experienced when you travel. The best "finds" are often made at the most unexpected times and places. So, if you travel by car, go prepared to carry back anything you might happen to acquire. Of course, you will get off the freeway and onto out-of-the-way country roads. This is where the interest is. Whoever heard of anyone having anything interesting happen to him on a freeway? But, on the back roads, the most delightful things can happen to you—and do.

One lady, while riding along a back road, noticed a bonfire in a field behind some farm buildings. There, standing dangerously near the flames and looking very much threatened, was what appeared to be a tall cupboard. Letting out a gasp, indicating that her husband should throw on the brakes, she jumped out of the car, climbed through a barbed-wire fence, and ran to the site. Sure enough! A man and a boy were burning "Jes' sum ol' stuff 'n' things nobudy wants." The items had been collecting dirt and mouse tracks for years in a shed they now needed to store some grain in " 'til the price gits up." Much to the amazement of the owner, the woman paid him eleven dollars, and the three of them carried the rescued cupboard back and secured it atop the Volkwagen. The woman went triumphantly on her way. The cupboard now stands proudly and handsomely refinished displaying an *almost* full set of English Staffordshire ware purchased at a country auction.

If you persist, you can still find a bonanza of items with all kinds of possibilities—off the beaten track. An old Boston rocker in which someone is rocking on a front porch may be available if you put on your most folksy manner. But be genuine. Don't be pushy, and don't be in a hurry. Inquire, not about the chair at first, but about the family. And be prepared to listen. It may take a while; it isn't every day someone asks her those questions. In the course of the conversation, you may

Bits of fabric collected for years become a quilt, window drapery, cushions, dolls, and wall decorations. Do-it-yourself storage, platform bed, and a bold striped floor complete this room for fun and for sleeping. *Courtesy: Syroco.*

discover that the owner of the rocker has an attic where three generations of family relics have been stashed. If you work it just right, she may invite you to follow her through the kitchen and up a creaky stairway. Who knows what a junk hunter's paradise you may find or what treasure you may carry away. But don't be surprised if she won't part with the Boston rocker, "until I finish ma settin'."

Don't be discouraged if you make some bad buys at first. The novice will undoubtedly bring home a lot of *real* junk to begin with, but after a few years of study and perseverance, the rewards of junking will delight you. And the once-beautiful articles that you salvage and restore can add a personal charm and character that will make your home distinctly yours.

16
Housework-- Drudgery or Therapy

The most discouraging thing about housework is that the things that show are the things *you don't do.* Think about it! If everything is spic 'n' span all the time, the house is straight, beds are made, dishes are clean and in the cupboard, clothes washed, dried, and put away, everyone just accepts this as the normal state of things. But try leaving all this undone for just one day and see the reaction you get from family members when they come home!

A Homemaker's Greatest Challenge

The biggest challenge for the twenty-four-hour homemaker is to accomplish the many daily tasks required to maintain a reasonably well-organized home, and at the same time to preserve a fair degree of self-pride and dignity and a feeling of accomplishment.

The first requisite to achieving this seemingly impossible feat is to avoid thinking of housework as drudgery. If you stop to count all the mundane tasks that must be repeated day after day, week in and week out, you could go stark staring mad! Instead, think of the reason for keeping a home. Concentrate on the purpose of it all. There is nothing demeaning about creating and maintaining a home for those you love most; on the contrary, it can be the most rewarding achievement of your life.

Because the physical environment has such a powerful influence upon the lives of families, you should make creating the best possible home environment your first priority. Strive to establish an environment in which every family member can find refuge and security and can function at his or her best. The answer is not dollars but a sincere desire. Be positive; try to think of the day-to-day routine as a work of love. Think of what Kahlil Gibran in his well known book, *The Prophet,* says: "Work is love made visible." As you go about your daily tasks, remind yourself that through what you are doing you are expressing your love to those who mean the most to you.

How many times have you heard it said, "What good does a college education do for someone who spends life doing the tedious and routine tasks required in keeping a home and caring for a family?" I say, "Never is a college education more important or needed more than in being a homemaker or mother." Your mind is free to expand while your hands are busy with mundane chores.

There are many positive aspects of housework to think about. Remember that in your home you are your own boss. No one is standing over you telling you what to do. If you don't want to do something today, don't do it! Put it off for another time. No one will know the difference but you. The only deadlines are those you set yourself and there ought not to be many of these lest they regulate your life and take precedence over more important projects. For example, a certain amount of planning is necessary, but a rigid adherence to a schedule can conflict with important family projects that invariably arise. And after all, what is your home all about?

As you go about your work, think about something you have been reading. Plan the talk you were asked to give in PTA. Turn on the news to keep abreast of current issues. Listen; it will help you form intelligent opinions. Put on a tape or a record, either a familiar one that you enjoy, or a Beethoven or Mozart or whatever you would like to know better. The mind's horizons are boundless, and you can turn housework into therapy if you make the effort. It may take some discipline initially, but soon it can become a habit.

Count Your Blessings

To avoid those early morning blues, begin each day by looking for something to lift your spirits. Look for beauty. It is all around you. If it is a drab February day, pull back the curtains and observe the rhythm of bare branches against the grey sky. Maybe a single sparrow is perched there. Have you ever noticed the subtle beauty in his unobtrusive little feathers? When you go down to the kitchen, throw out some dry crumbs. The bread box needs cleaning anyway, so take five minutes to do it.

Nowhere does positive thinking pay off more than in your own home. As you pass the front door and see the matted, worn carpet, don't bemoan the fact that you can't afford to replace it now because the money has to go to pay the dentist for Johnny's braces. Instead, pause a second and be glad that the children are at home and that you have friendly neighbors.

When you get to the kitchen and see the cupboard piled with last night's dishes, don't throw up your hands—pause and be grateful that you have enough food to require that many dishes. And be glad that your children feel free to bring their friends home to raid the larder.

Respite—Especially for Mother

When breakfast is over and everyone has gone, treat yourself to a few minutes of peace and quiet. "Ha!" you say. "That sounds fine, but what about that demanding two-year-old?" I say, "Put him in a playpen and toss him some safe toys." If this has been a regular routine, he will enjoy it and accept it without protest. Now get your favorite magazine or that book you have put off reading, take the phone off the hook, sit down, put your feet up, and relax. So, the doorbell rings! Let it ring! If it is something of importance, the person will return. If it isn't, you don't want whoever it is to know you are home anyway. When you have pulled yourself together, you can attack the day with new ideas and a fresh vigor, and probably you can do twice as much in half the time.

I am not overlooking the fact that mothers of young children live constantly on the brink of disaster and that full concentration for very long is impossible. Falls, spills, and backyard squabbles call you to the rescue frequently and regularly, and you must run on a moment's notice. This fact, however, should not completely dominate your waking hours. Wise planning for home safety can eliminate most mishaps, and backyard squabbles often work out better without parental intervention.

It is imperative that the twenty-four-hour homemaker and mother of young children have some daily relief from the preschool mentality that she is locked into. *Where* she goes or what she does is not important, but *that* she goes *is* important. An hour by herself behind closed doors, to nap, to read, to scream, or to just sit and stare at the wall may do the trick.

Meet Realities Head On

In the normal process of day-to-day living, a certain amount of accumulated clutter in a house is inevitable.

"Well, you asked what I do all day."

It is folly to think otherwise. But with a little cooperation, this can be handled without undue effort. Organize the household members to do specific chores. Start when children are toddlers, and they will form helpful habits as they grow up. Mothers who work out of the home find this a necessity. But full-time homemakers should do the same. Not only will it help, but these habits will stand the children in good stead throughout their lives.

To avoid unnecessary frustration, anticipate the realities of family living together. Children drop muddy boots where they take them off, so place a box near the back door for this purpose. Toys and games have a way of scattering themselves around where "nobody" left them. Don't make a big thing of it. Just toss them in a box placed in some central location.

Is dusting one of your least favorite jobs? Then don't make yourself miserable thinking you have to do it every day. So a little dust does accumulate! Whisk off big flat wood surfaces when they need it badly. Keep a feather duster handy. It is a marvelous household tool. With it, you can redistribute the dust in a minute if someone is coming.

Then there are those three meals a day! On days when you are late or don't know what you are going to have for dinner, set the table before anyone gets home. Fix a centerpiece with something from the backyard or the crisper, and when the family arrives it will appear to them that dinner is ready, and any delay will never be noticed. This really works!

Tricks for Preventing Frustration

- The adage that "a stitch in time saves nine" is never more true than in referring to the little mishaps that frequently occur around the house. Be alert to the little things that, when taken care of immediately with a minimum of effort, can prevent a major task later on.
- Spills are inevitable, so anticipate them by having a stain and spot removal book and the necessary equipment in a box or basket in a convenient place—but keep it out of the reach of young children.
- In a handy place, keep household brochures on carpet, fabric, furniture, and floor care. Include a good supply of "how-to" brochures; you never can tell

when you might be struck by the urge to make something useful.

- Do little jobs at unexpected times. While you talk on the telephone, wipe off the woodwork around the door, polish the chrome on the refrigerator, wash a window, prepare vegetables, or do whatever needs doing that is within reach of your *long* cord—get a shoulder rest for your phone if you don't have one.
- Don't waste time hunting for things. Get a good-sized notebook and label it "Where did I put it?" Whenever you put something away that you may not need for a while, enter it in the book. (Be sure to keep the book in the same place so you won't have to hunt for that too!) When seasonal items are needed, you want last year's fishing hat, or you need that third-grade halloween costume for Martha, you just whip out your little book, and with one quick look you see where you put it. No hunting, no irritation. Try it! It just may be one of the greatest time and frustration savers you have ever tried.
- Be realistic about daily wear and tear. Let modern technology serve you. Select home furnishing items with practicality in mind. But remember, practicality does not mean drabness.
- Always be ready for a change of pace. Take advantage of an unexpected impulse. Some of your best cleaning may be done at the most unlikely times. At the end of a particularly frustrating day, when children and other family members have gone to bed but you can't settle down to read or relax, cook up a batch of fudge (if chocolate is your weakness) and attack some cleaning job you have been dreading and putting off. The fudge will give you quick energy, and with no interruptions you can zip through a miserable task in a way that you didn't dream was possible. When you begin to feel physically tired, take a warm bath and fall into bed. When morning comes, you will be so pleased with yourself that the day will get off to a good start.
- Don't wear your house out cleaning it! All it will get you is a tired back and a bad disposition, and your family will suffer for it. Let things mellow a little. So the windows have rain spots on them. If you clean them, it will only storm again. Clean them occasionally, but in between look *beyond* them, not *at* them.
- Do those things first that for the least effort make the biggest showing. A bed can be made in a minute, and what a difference it makes. If you have an upstairs, you are lucky: beds can wait.
- Let your head save your heels. Cultivate the habit of assembling items to go upstairs, or from one part of the house to the other. Don't make a trip with each little thing.
- Don't worry about keeping a sparkle on your seldom-used china and crystal. What's so bad about a little dust. Wash them when you need them. Who is going to care whether or not they are washed regularly? Put your effort where it shows.

You can undoubtedly add endless items to this list. Do! And remind yourself of them periodically. Any way to save time or prevent irritation is worth thinking about.

Putting Values in True Perspective

Put your values in the right perspective. Set your priorities. Don't allow yourself to feel caught in a web of household chores. A certain amount of order is absolutely necessary, but let your house look lived in. No one is comfortable in a home that is too tidy or new looking. There is a little wooden plaque that reads, "My house is clean enough to be healthy and dirty enough to be happy." Hang it for all to see. Certainly your family will not remember when they come home every Tuesday that the floor was freshly polished or that the washing was done and put away. What they will remember is the mood you were in when they came home, that your hair was combed, that you had something interesting to say, and that you took time to listen to them.

Concentrate on activities that will enrich your life and the lives of your family. You will be a happier person and a better homemaker. Occasionally do what you *want* to do and not what you think you *ought* to do. It will do something good for your feeling of individual freedom. Remind yourself every once in a while that what others have and how others live should not be a measure for you and your family. The notion of keeping up with the Joneses should have been abandoned long ago. This idea has caused far too much unhappiness and anxiety for too many people. Instead, plan and live your own life your own way. And the Joneses? So what!

17
Tips for Saving Energy

Although we have touched upon the need to preserve energy in our homes, the critical importance of this subject justifies closer attention. The way Americans live requires an astonishing amount of energy, and although experts disagree on how long our sources will last, we are using energy faster than nature can create it.

In the past, energy seemed inexhaustible and was so inexpensive that we made no effort to save it. Now we are well on our way to exhausting our known resources, and it is essential that we adjust our everyday living standards to conserve energy in all forms.

We *can* slow down our consumption of energy and still live very well. We must begin by changing our attitudes and values; breaking old habits and developing new ones. Learning how much energy we *must* use and what is wasteful is the first step. Learn to read the gas and electric meters. Set a goal of energy use for your home, then check the meters regularly to see if you are reducing consumption to stay within that goal. This will demand changes in almost every aspect of your life—time, effort, and financial resources. The key is careful management, which means using available resources in the most effective way to obtain the maximum comfort and convenience.

There are many ways to conserve energy in and around the home without sacrificing to any great extent our standard of living. Reducing the amount of energy means saving money that becomes available for other needs. Although some of the energy-saving devices may involve spending money, the long-range benefits achieved will more than pay for the cost.

Insulation: Some Questions and Answers

Most homes built when energy was plentiful and cheap did not have enough insulation, but insulation can be

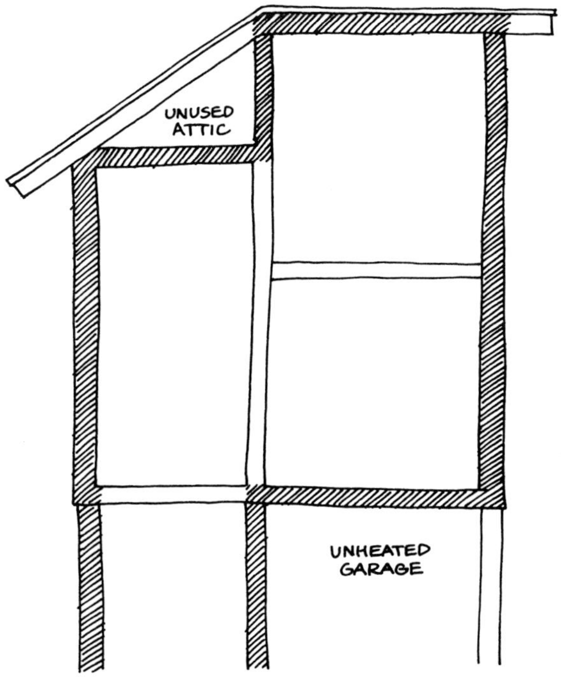

Insulation belongs behind *every* floor, ceiling, and wall that joins an unheated or uncovered area—in the attic at the floorline if the attic's not used, overhead if it is used; in outer walls that adjoin unheated areas; in ceilings and dormers of heated rooms if there's no attic above; in floors over unheated cellars and crawl spaces; in cellar walls if the basement is used for living space.

Types of Insulation

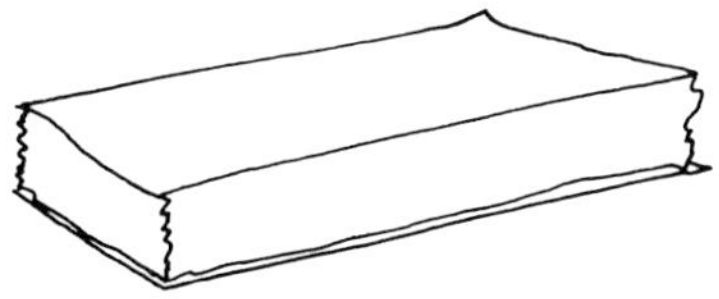

Batt

Loose fill

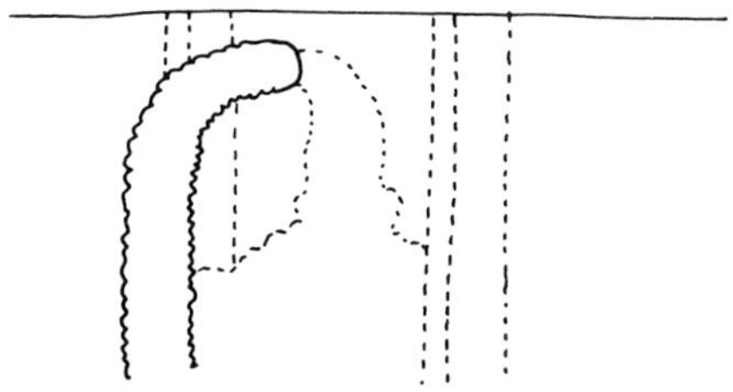

Foam (blown in)

added to almost any house. Whether you are building, remodelling, or just planning to conserve energy in your present home, the place to begin is with insulation. Perhaps no step is as simple or pays better returns in conserving energy and dollars than the proper installation of adequate and efficient insulation in your home.

Exactly what is insulation?

Insulation is a material that helps to keep cool air *out* in the winter and *in* in the summer.

Where should you insulate?

Insulation belongs under every floor, above every ceiling, and in every wall that joins an unheated area. Generally the homeowner can insulate an attic floor, where savings generally will be the greatest.

What kind of insulation should you use?

There are four types of insulation from which to choose:

- Blankets are rolls of fiberglass insulation with or without vapor barriers.
- Batts are similar to blankets but are cut into four- or eight-foot lengths.
- "Loose Fill" usually refers to wool or cellulose fiber meant to be poured onto the attic floor or into wells.
- "Blown-in" refers to wool or cellulose fiber that is blown into an attic or wall by a pneumatic blower.

The kind of insulation you choose should depend upon your type of heating fuel, your house style, and the level of existing insulation, if any.

How much insulation should you use?

The amount of insulation used should depend upon the *type* of insulation chosen, *where* it will be installed, and the *climate*.

The effectiveness of insulation is indicated by the "R" factor—a measure of resistance to heat flow. The

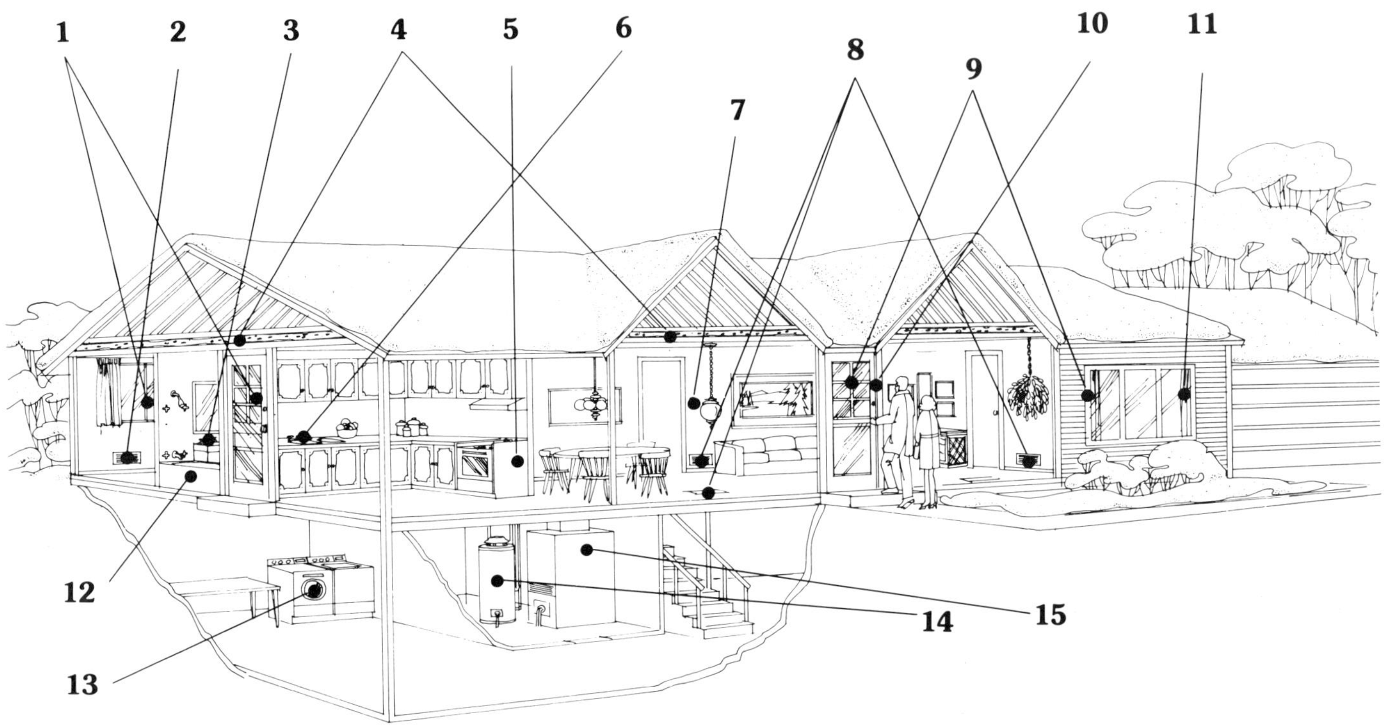

Conservation is a family affair: (1) Install storm doors and windows. (2) Close heating registers and doors to unused rooms. (3) Don't keep hot water running while shaving. (4) Insulate over top-floor ceilings to 6-inch thickness. (5) Match the gas flame to the size of the pan, and use a lid. (6) Be sure water faucets don't drip. (7) During waking hours leave your thermostat set at a comfortable temperature. Lower at night to a comfortable sleeping temperature. (8) Keep all heat outlets and air-return registers free from obstruction. (9) Check weatherstripping around doors and windows, and caulk outside cracks. (10) Keep opening of windows and outside doors to a minimum. (11) Open curtains, blinds, and drapes to let the sunshine in. Close them at night. (12) A shower takes approximately half as much water as a bath. (13) Clean the lint screen of your dryer after each load. (14) Your water heater should be set at 110° or "normal" temperature. Drain about 1 or 2 gallons of water from the bottom tap each month. (15) Change or clean your furnace filter every 60 days.
Courtesy of Mountain Fuel.

higher the R rating, the more effective the insulation. Remember that not all brands of insulative materials have the same thermal resistance, so stick with the R factor. Your dealer will have a chart showing the insulation values of all insulating materials; for example, urea formaldehyde foam has the highest R value per square inch—4.8. Loose-fill vermiculite has the lowest R value—2.1 per square inch.

Can you insulate your own home?

Often you can do your own insulating, particularly in the attic floor. If you decide to do the work yourself, consult your local building supplier. He or she will advise you as to the best type of insulation for your home and area, will help you estimate the amount you will need, and will furnish you the necessary equipment. To assure a professional job, follow the instructions printed on the product. The blankets, batts, and loose-fill types can be do-it-yourself projects, but the blow-in type requires a pneumatic blower, so you will probably need a professional contractor. If you decide to hire a contractor, your gas or utility company will recommend a reputable person. Or consult friends, or look through the yellow pages.

Before signing a contract, ask some pertinent questions. Have a clear understanding of the job to be done. Be sure the right amount of insulation is used. All insulative brands of materials should have printed on the bag the federal government specifications and Underwriters Laboratory test specifications along with the weight per bag and coverage. The average figure gives you a means of knowing how many bags a contractor should blow into your attic to achieve a particular R factor. Later, when the job is being done, count the number of bags actually used to make sure you are getting the amount of insulation specified. Make sure your contractor's employees are insured, and sign

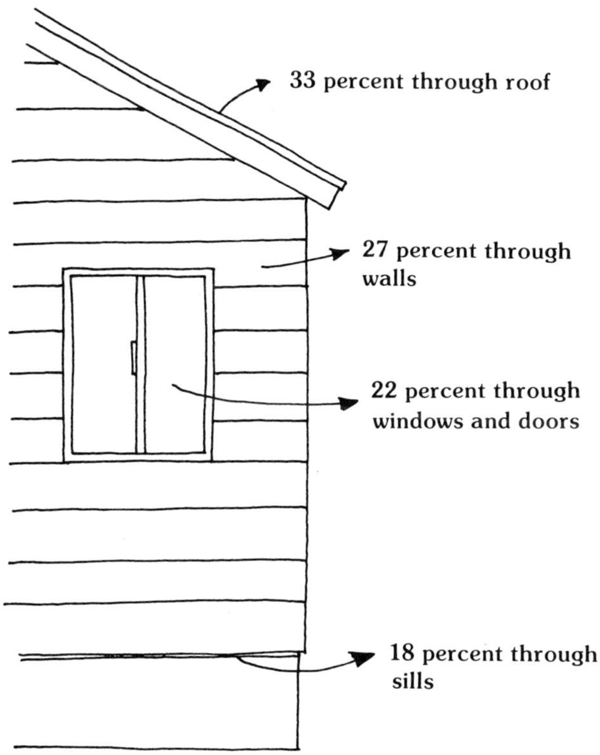

Heat loss in an uninsulated home.

the contract only when you are fully satisfied that it details everything you want. This does not mean you don't trust your contractor, it avoids any misunderstanding or disappointment.

Tightening Up the Ship—Air Leaks

Some exchange of air in and out of a house is unavoidable, but excessive movement of air can account for a very large portion of your annual fuel bill. In a well-insulated house, the largest source of energy loss can be the air leaks around windows and doors and through other cracks and small openings.

Storm windows and storm doors

Storm windows and storm doors cut heat loss (or heat gain) at these points about in half. Insulating glass (two panes of glass sealed together at the edges) has approximately the same effect. Triple glazing (insulating glass plus a storm window) is even more effective and often is used in extremely cold climates.

Storm windows and doors can be installed by a contractor or a skilled homeowner. Using pre-hung doors, which are already assembled to frames, makes the job easier.

Plastic sheeting, available in hardware stores, makes effective storm windows. It should be stretched and stapled to a wooden frame that is slightly smaller than the inside window frame. Then the frame should be lined with a foam weatherstripping material, so that it will fit snugly against the window frame.

According to the National Bureau of Standards, an investment in storm windows will pay for itself in a decade.

Weatherstripping

Weatherstripping can be installed by anyone of average do-it-yourself capability. Many different types are available; felt strips, foam rubber, flexible vinyl, spring bronze, and others. A flexible vinyl tubing is usually regarded as the best material. The advice of a knowledgeable hardware store salesman will help in making a choice. Instruction sheets generally are included in the package.

Window sashes and doors should be weatherstripped on all sides and tops and bottoms. Do not overlook the meeting rail where the top and bottom sash of double-hung windows come together.

Entrance doors should be well weatherstripped, as should attic doors, inside and outside basement doors, and doors on furnace rooms. Any door between a heated space and an unheated space should be weatherstripped.

Caulking

Caulking is a simple do-it-yourself job. Caulking guns and materials are inexpensive and are available at all

Where caulking is needed.

hardware stores. Oil or resin base compound is the least expensive material, but it is less durable than latex, butyl, and polyvinyl. Your dealer will advise you as to which type is the best for your particular purpose.

Caulking should be applied outside around windows and door frames and wherever two different materials or parts of the house meet.

While you are inspecting for all possible leaks, check the putty on your windows. It may need replacing.

Thresholds

You may be losing heating and cooling energy dollars as well as admitting dust, noise, and moisture under outside doors. A threshold could solve the problem. The threshold requires only a hammer and screwdriver to set it in place. Caulk the ends for water protection.

As a heating source, *a fireplace can be deceptive.* A burning fire generates a large flow of air through the hearth and up the chimney. Although the immediate air is heated, the rest of the house is being cooled. For maximum savings while using the fireplace, close the doors to the rest of the house and turn the thermostat down to keep the furnace from working. When the fireplace is not in use, keep the damper tightly closed.

To capture more of the fire's heat before it goes up the flue, you can add an air heating grate, a do-it-yourself project which not only holds the burning wood but also forces warm air into the room. Detailed directions are available from the "National Center for Appropriate Technology," P.O. Box 3838, Butte, Montana 59701. Your local plumber can help you with the installation.

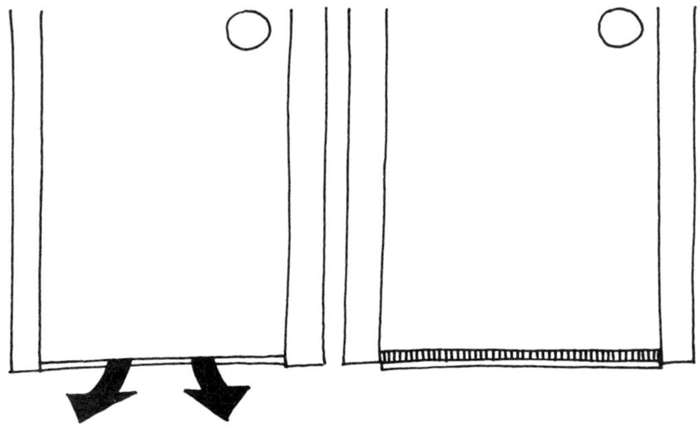

A threshold keeps out cold, heat, and noise.

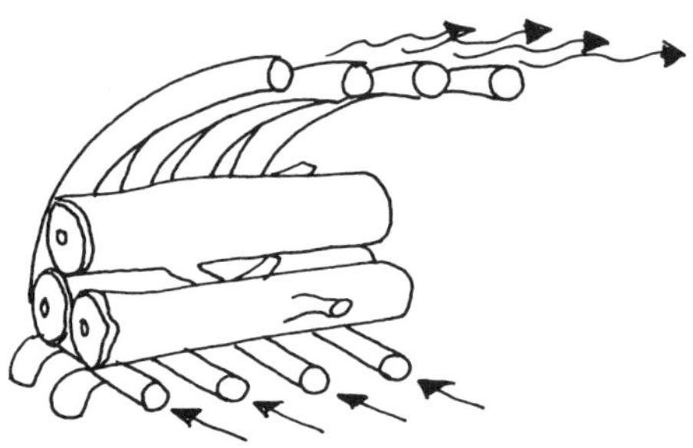

A practical do-it-yourself heat saver.

Heating and Cooling

The biggest waste of energy is the loss of heated air through walls, ceilings, floors, and windows. Adequate insulation, storm windows and doors, and weather-stripping help, but there are many other things you can do to get maximum efficiency from your present heating system, regardless of the type of fuel being used; at the same time you can increase the comfort in your home at less cost.

Set thermostat at a comfortable setting (68°–70°) and leave it alone. Turn it lower at night but not so low as to cause the heating system to work overtime to reheat your house in the morning. For greatest efficiency the thermostat should be located, not in corridors, but in rooms most frequently used.

When you are going to be away for several days, turn the thermostat to about 45°.

Keep air filters in furnace and heat pumps, and keep radiators and baseboard heaters clean at all times.

The right humidity in your home can increase your comfort. Since you will be more comfortable at a lower temperature where the humidity is right, you save energy. A humidifier is a wise investment, but a pan of water located near a heating outlet will do essentially the same thing. For an efficient air-conditioning unit, select one that is the proper size for the space to be cooled.

Prevent Hot Water Wasters

One of the worst offenders in wasting hot water and energy is a leaky faucet, so repair it immediately. Drips soon add up to gallons. Accumulate dishes until the dishwasher is filled; avoid wasting hot water by leaving it running continuously while washing and rinsing dishes; wash only full loads of laundry; use heated water only in the wash cycle; use water no hotter than necessary; insulate hot water pipes and your hot water tank; drain the sediment from the bottom of your hot water tank once a year.

Dry Efficiently

Clean the lint trap of your dryer before each use; avoid over drying or drying only one or two items at a time; don't overload the dryer; dry similar items together to prevent over or underdrying; vent your dryer to the outside; remove the load promptly when dry or not quite dry to avoid wrinkling; use an outdoor line for drying whenever possible; reduce ironing to a minimum by selecting drip-dry garments, household linens, and other fabrics.

Pot too big **Pot just right** **Pot too small**

A utensil that fits the heating element saves fuel.

Cooking and Baking Energy-Saving Tricks

Defrost food before cooking to save fuel; use cooking utensils that fit the unit; keep units clean; make more use of your pressure cooker to cut cooking time; where appropriate, use tight-fitting lids; use flat-bottomed pans; reduce heat as soon as boiling begins and turn off as soon as cooking is finished.

When *baking,* plan your meals to use oven to capacity; preheat oven only when required and no longer than necessary; don't be an "oven-peeper"—this wastes heat; turn off oven promptly when baking is completed or a few moments before. Never use an open oven as a room heater.

Refrigerate and Freeze Economically

Avoid locating a refrigerator near the range or near a hot air duct; allow for air circulation behind and below the refrigerator; keep condenser coils clean; don't allow frost to accumulate more than ¼ inch thick—it uses more electricity; be sure the door is airtight; avoid opening more than necessary; partially cool your hot food before refrigerating; don't place uncovered liquids in the refrigerator; the vapors they give off add to the compressor's workload.

The freezer should be treated the same as the refrigerator. Remember that a freezer is more efficient when reasonably full, and check your freezer periodically to make sure it is working properly.

Lighting Offenders

Every little bit helps, so turn off unnecessary lights indoors and out; reduce lighting levels where practical; as much as possible, do tasks that require high level of illumination during daylight hours; keep lighting fixtures clean. Use fluorescent lighting whenever possible; it produces about four times as much light per watt as do incandescent bulbs.

The reflective surfaces of the home can add materially to light efficiency. Therefore, in choosing colors for your home to conserve energy, select light colors, they will reflect the light, and your rooms will require a lower level of illumination. Consider the new sodium vapor lights for outdoors. They consume less energy for a given light output and have a longer life. Long-life bulbs emit less light than standard incandescent bulbs of the same wattage, so use them only in hard-to-reach places.

Where lamps and fixtures have two or more sockets for incandescent bulbs, consider using a single large bulb in only one socket. A 100 watt bulb will produce 50 percent more light than four 25-watt bulbs for the same amount of energy. When possible, locate portable and hanging lamps in a corner to reflect light from two wall surfaces instead of one. Use lampshades with a white liner to reflect the maximum of light but keep them sufficiently dense to hide the bulb.

Other Ways of Saving Energy in the Home

Whether you own your own home, rent a house, or live in an apartment or a trailer, there are numerous simple ways to save energy and money. A constant evaluation of our daily use of resources can make us aware of the necessity of using only the amount of energy we *really* need.

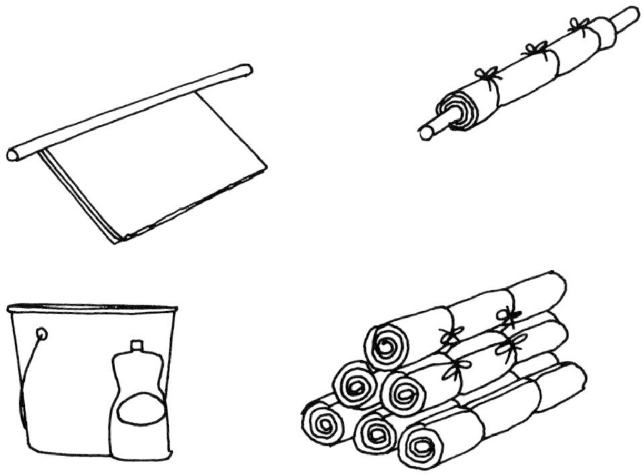

Logs from newspapers. Roll newspapers on section of old broom handle. Soak in water with a little detergent. Remove stick. Allow rolls to dry.

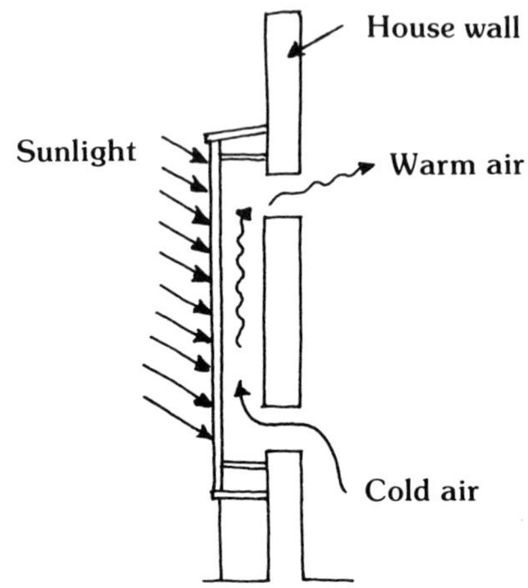

Wall heater (side view)

Following are some additional ways to cut down on energy use in our homes:

- Provide adequate ventilation for a good flow of air in the attic.
- Keep doors and windows closed while the air conditioner is operating. Don't attempt to cool the outdoors.
- Keep your house well painted. A good coat of paint seals small cracks. In climates where heat is your biggest concern, use white paint to reflect light and heat and thus reduce the heat build-up in your home.
- Check small openings. Be sure the mail chute closes tightly.
- Close off unused rooms.
- Open windows on cool days and nights, and close them tightly during hot days.
- Install awnings on sunny exposures to keep the sun from striking the glass.
- Close drapery to keep heat *out* in the summer and keep heat *in* in winter.
- Use insulated drapery or insulated linings.
- Take showers rather than baths. Showers use about half as much water.
- Dress appropriately: warm clothes in winter and light airy clothes in summer.
- Use more hand tools instead of electric ones, such as carving knives, hedge clippers, and lawn mowers. When you use power tools, keep them sharp. They will cut faster and use less energy.
- Make your own fertilizer from leaves, lawn clippings, and garbage by building a compost pile. Commercial fertilizer takes energy to make.
- Make paper logs from old newspapers. Soak several papers in water to which a little detergent has been added. Roll them on a section of an old broom handle. Remove the stick and allow the rolls to dry in the house. The furnace room is a good place. The moisture will help fight winter dryness. When once dry, paper logs burn much like wood: they are clean, leave almost no ash, and are real energy savers. Add to them regularly to maintain a supply. Finding a good use for accumulating papers is an extra bonus.
- If you have radiators, make reflectors to get more heat. A piece of sheet metal, or aluminum foil taped to the wall or glued to a piece of plasterboard and placed behind the radiator will reflect the heat into the room.
- Let the sun work for you in the winter. Draw back the drapery and lift the awnings.
- Consider solar heating. You can make a window heater by using your existing windows or build in a wall heater. The directions for these may be obtained by writing to the National Center for Appropriate Technology, P.O. Box 3838, Butte, Montana 59701.
- When building a house, use the natural landscape for maximum weatherproofing. Use the ground as an insulator. Put the windows where they will do the most good.
- Plant shade trees to protect roof and windows. You will ease the workload of your cooling system. A wind break of trees will reduce wind in winter and cut your heating bill.

When You Shop—Save Energy

- Buy long-lasting products. Less frequent replacements mean money and energy savings. Look for the guarantees.
- Consider the long-range cost of operating a product—not just the initial cost.
- Use recyclable containers such as glass, aluminum, steel and paper, and turn them in at a recycling center.
- Buy recycled products. These can be real values.
- Shop for second-hand appliances. With a little study, you can recycle them yourself.

What may appear to be a very small saving of energy in the average household can add up to sizable savings in the country as a whole. If every family makes a concerted effort to save energy by every possible means, no matter how small, it will help our nation to alleviate the present energy crisis, while our technologists are finding new sources of energy to meet our ever growing needs.

Reference Materials

Magazines like *Popular Mechanics, Popular Science, Mechanix Illustrated,* and *Family Handyman* often have articles on things people can do to save energy. You can look through these magazines at your library. While there, you could also ask your librarian for the latest books on home energy conservation.

Contact the local Extension Service of your state University and your county agent. They may have brochures and booklets with helpful information. You can get booklets like these:

- *How to Set Up a Coal or Wood Stove,* a 2-page brochure, and *Home Heating in an Emergency,* a 15-page booklet. Single copies of both are available free from the Cooperative Extension Service University of New Hampshire, Durham, NH 03824
- *Making the Most of Your Energy Dollars in Home Heating and Cooling,* a 16-page booklet with information about insulation and the cost savings possible with energy conservation in the home. Single copies are available free from Publications Office, National Bureau of Standards, Washington, DC 20234.
- *A Community Planning Guide to Weatherization,* a 37-page booklet that explains how to set up a cost-effective weatherization program in your neighborhood. Single copies are available free from Community Services Administration, Washington, DC 20506.
- *The Fuel Savers: A Kit of Solar Ideas for Existing Homes,* a 60-page booklet with ideas and drawings for do-it-yourself solar heating projects. Copies are available for $3.50 from NORWESCAP, Inc., Prospect St., Phillipsburg, NJ 08865.
- *Save Money: Save Energy!* National Center for Appropriate Technology, P.O. Box 3838, Butte, MT 59701.

Contact the utilities companies in your area. They will have free booklets with the latest materials and methods for saving energy in your home.

18
And in Conclusion

At a time when our national values are being challenged both at home and abroad, more than ever before our country needs the strength and stability of the home to maintain and foster the dependable and eternal values upon which our nation was established. If we heed the findings of the environmental scientists—who emphasize the importance of the physical environment upon the formation of attitudes and character development during the formative years—we will set as top priority the responsibility for creating home environments in honesty, integrity, tolerance, understanding, vitality, and industry are nurtured and preserved.

A home is to live in, a place in which to find security and self-fulfillment. Home is where each of us develops his or her individuality. It is where we learn to eat, to speak, to dress, and to relate to other people. Home is where we learn to do some of the important tasks of living and where we do what we *want* to do when we don't *have* to do anything. Home is where we acquire the culture that makes us what we are and where we expand to our full growth and capability through day to day living.

Home should be the place where interests and values are established, and goals developed, where children learn to appreciate good books, music, and art, and where they learn respect and love for others. A well-designed physical environment can help set the proper emotional climate for children to grow in and for adults to live in comfortably, and it is *not* dependent upon cost. But it does not happen by accident; it requires intelligent and insightful planning and constant revision. Such planning and revision will inevitably pay big dividends by providing a home in which normal activities may be carried on with a minimum of discord.

The Art of Gentle Living

Having put so much love and effort into creating your home, do you know how to enjoy it? Have you been so busy creating the environment that you have forgotten to develop the art of living in it? How does one acquire the art of gentle living?

From the English, the people of that little island where more Americans have their roots than any other single country, we can learn the art of gentle living. The house with the "well-bred English look" has had universal appeal since its inception some four hundred years ago. The English house has the look of a home that is lived in but well cared for. Nothing looks new, nothing looks "decorated." Comfort more than any other thing is what one senses upon entering. A comfortable chair with a good light, books dropped with visible markers—suggesting someone's return—and a tiny vase of freshly picked flowers invite you to linger. What does one know of good living who creates rooms that become disrupted when books are left lying about? Such "flawless" rooms may have a dazzling visual impact, but they are not for living.

The Importance of Beauty in Our Lives

What of beauty in your home environment? Is it a necessary ingredient? Yes! The therapeutic value that beauty can have in our lives cannot be overestimated. To create beauty is to care about how you live. And to care about how you live means enriching your own and your family's way of life—and the lives of all who come within the walls of your home. If you have beautiful things in your home, use them and enjoy them. If you have fine china and silver, don't keep them stored behind closed doors. Take them out and use them, not just for company but for your family—at least some of the time. Teach children to take pride in eating at a tastefully set table and to recognize a salad fork. Teach them how to care for nice things and to appreciate the family heirlooms you may have. True, we must not let the acquiring and love of "things" loom too large in our lives, but to live with objects of beauty and take pride in caring for them can add to our pleasure and refinement, strengthen our ties to the past, and add significance to our daily lives.

Beauty is by no means confined to items of monetary value. In fact, beauty has no price tag. It is everywhere, available to everyone. We need only to learn to see it. To see beauty in commonplace things is one of life's great challenges. Elizabeth Gordon, former editor of *House Beautiful,* said of beauty, "If you can't afford it when you are poor, you won't likely have it when you are rich."

Home—A Haven of Security

Today's home environment should be a blending of the best from our cherished past and the best of our abundant present in a way suitable to your life style. A home in which there is warmth and true hospitality reflects your own sincere way of living. True hospitality cannot be turned on at will, and pretending to be what we are not impresses nobody. Love of people and a genuine desire to share the security of your home must come from within. It is this love more than any other that makes the difference between a house and a home. Certainly the difference has nothing to do with the amount of money expended.

With the mounting pressures in modern life, the turmoil of our bulging cities, where much of our time is spent in crowded subways, buses, and elevators or queuing up for services, it is essential that our homes be true havens, providing a feeling of security and well-being for each family member. True peace may come from within, but we need all the help we can get from our environment to nurture and preserve that peace.

Human beings function at their best in an atmosphere free from irritation and frustration. The conscious and constant refining in our daily lives can contribute immeasurably to a feeling of tranquility and repose. As families change, their needs change; and searching out the best solutions to these changing needs is a constant challenge. Let your house reflect your varied interests in books, music, hobbies, and religion. In your home, in everything you have and everything you do, maintain a sense of appropriateness to your way of life, a suitability. Someone said, "A man's home is a reflection of the way he lives and thinks." Could it be that as our home is, so will we live and think?

General Readings

Allen, Phyllis Sloan. *Beginnings of Interior Environment.* Provo, Utah: Brigham Young University Press, 1977. A survey of domestic architecture and an introduction to all areas of interior design.

Alexander, Mary Jean. *Decorating Made Simple.* New York: Doubleday and Company, Inc., 1964.

Better Homes and Gardens Decorating Book, 2d ed. Des Moines: Meredith Corporation, 1975.

Birren, Faber. *Light, Color and Environment.* New York: Van Nostrand Reinhold Company, 1969.

Collins, Peggie Varney, and Shirley Wright Collins. *Putting It All Together: A Consumer's Guide to Home Furnishings.* New York: Charles Scribner's Sons, 1977.

Complete Home Catalog. New York: Bantam Books, 1977.

Faulkner, Ray, and Sarah Faulkner. *Inside Today's Home.* New York: Holt, Rinehart and Winston, 1975. Covers all aspects of interior design, including period furniture styles.

Good Housekeeping Decorating and Do-It-Yourself. London: Hearst Corporation, 1977. Very practical; includes do-it-yourself projects.

How to Make Your Windows Beautiful. Sturgis, Michigan: Kirsch Company. Published by a manufacturer of curtain rods. This volume illustrates and explains all the window types, various ways of treating them, and hardware for each type.

Maass, John. *The Gingerbread Age.* New York: Bramhall House, 1957. A view of Victorian America.

Royal Barry Wills Associates. *More Houses for Good Living.* New York: Architectural Book Publishing Company, 1968.

St. Marie, S. Satenig. *Homes Are for People.* New York: John Wiley and Sons, Inc., 1975.

Sulahria, Julie, and Ruby Diamond. *Inside Design: Creating Your Environment.* San Francisco: Canfield Press, 1977.

Whiton, Sherrill. *Interior Design and Decoration,* 4th ed. New York: J. B. Lippincott Company, 1974. Emphasizes period furnishings.

Wingate, Isabel, Karen Gillespie, and Betty Milgrom. *Know Your Merchandise.* New York: McGraw-Hill Book Company, 1975.

Wright, Frank Lloyd. *The Natural House.* New York· Bramhall House, 1954.

Other Readings

Catalogs and brochures from fabric designers and manufacturers.

Catalogs and brochures from furniture manufacturers.

Current periodicals such as *American Home, Better Homes and Gardens, House Beautiful, Interior Design, Women's Day, 101 Decorating Ideas, Housing, Professional Builder.*

Hudson Home Guides. Pleasantville, New York: Hudson Group.

- Building and Remodeling
- Custom Homes
- Kitchens, Baths, and Family Rooms
- Home Improvement
- Home Plans and Projects

Booklets advertised in periodicals.

- Planning aids
- How to. . . .
- Do it yourself
- Home improvement and repair
- Home furnishings and decoration
- Crafts and hobbies

Index